DIGGING UP
the Past

The *Titanic*

Essential Library

An Imprint of Abdo Publishing | www.abdopublishing.com

DIGGING UP the Past

The *Titanic*

BY LISA J. AMSTUTZ

CONTENT CONSULTANT
CAPTAIN CHARLES WEEKS
PROFESSOR EMERITUS IN MARINE TRANSPORTATION
MAINE MARITIME ACADEMY

www.abdopublishing.com

Published by Abdo Publishing, a division of ABDO, PO Box 398166, Minneapolis, Minnesota 55439. Copyright © 2015 by Abdo Consulting Group, Inc. International copyrights reserved in all countries. No part of this book may be reproduced in any form without written permission from the publisher. Essential Library™ is a trademark and logo of Abdo Publishing.

Printed in the United States of America, North Mankato, Minnesota
032014
092014

THIS BOOK CONTAINS RECYCLED MATERIALS

Cover Photo: AP Images
Interior Photos: AP Images, 2, 25; Ralph White/Corbis, 6, 28, 33, 34, 36, 38; Bettmann/Corbis, 9, 13; Red Line Editorial, 11; Shutterstock Images, 11, 17 (inset); iStockphoto/Thinkstock, 17; National Geographic Society/Corbis, 18, 44; Dorling Kindersley/DK Images, 21; Ira Schwarz/AP Images, 31; NOAA, 40; Lori Johnston/NOAA, 46; Michel Lipchitz/AP Images, 48; Mike Kullen/AP Images, 51; Fred Jewell/AP Images, 54; John Gibbins/San Diego Union-Tribune/AP Images, 57; Chris Melzer/dpa/Corbis, 60; NOAA/Institute for Exploration/University of Rhode Island, 63; Raymond Wong/National Geographic Image Collection/Glow Images, 67, 83; Tom Gannam/AP Images, 68; Gail Oskin/AP Images, 73; Peter Lennihan/AP Images, 74; Stanley Leary/AP Images, 77; Matt York/AP Images, 80; Peter Morrison/AP Images, 87; NOAA Handout/AP Images, 90; RMS Titanic, Inc./AP Images, 93; Toni Garriga/epa/Corbis, 97

Editor: Arnold Ringstad
Series Designer: Becky Daum

Library of Congress Control Number: 2014932252

Cataloging-in-Publication Data

Amstutz, Lisa J.
 The Titanic / Lisa J. Amstutz.
  p. cm. -- (Digging up the past)
Includes bibliographical references and index.
ISBN 978-1-62403-238-7
1. Titanic (Steamship)--Juvenile literature.   2. Shipwrecks--North Atlantic Ocean--Juvenile literature.   I. Title.
910--dc23
                                                        2014932252

CONTENTS

1

A Titanic Tragedy

All the scientists could see was mud. They had been staring at a video screen for nine days now, and mud was all they had found. Their eyes burned. Mind-numbing boredom had long since set in. Yet expedition leader Robert Ballard did not dare take his eyes off the screen for an instant. A vital clue could appear at any moment.

Ballard and his crew were the first people to see the *Titanic* in more than 70 years.

The American and French scientists, led by Ballard and Jean-Louis Michel, had already spent 56 days searching for the luxury ocean liner *Titanic*. The *Titanic* sank in 1912, and its location had been a mystery ever since. These scientists, working aboard their ship, hoped to find it. At first they had just used sonar, but now they were also using a high-tech deep-sea robotic camera sled called *Argo*. Video from *Argo* showed up on a monitor inside the boat. But the screen showed only mud. They were beginning to give up hope of finding the *Titanic*. Then, just before 1:00 a.m. on September 1, 1985, *Argo* pilot Stu Harris broke the silence. "There's something," he said, pointing to the screen. "It's coming in!"[1]

"Wreckage!" shouted researcher Bill Lange.[2] A chorus of whoops and hollers filled the control room as man-made objects streamed across the video monitor. The researchers knew these artifacts belonged to the *Titanic*. After 73 long years, the *Titanic* had been found! It was a dramatic story, a fitting sequel to the drama that played out decades earlier on the same stretch of ocean.

THE SINKING OF THE RMS *TITANIC*

"*Titanic* Sinks Four Hours after Hitting Iceberg" screamed the *New York Times* headline on April 16, 1912.[3] The news shocked the world. Frantic families on both sides of the Atlantic Ocean searched for news of their loved

Initial news reports underestimated the total number of deaths from the sinking.

ones. "I have bought two or three papers a day in the hope of seeing his name among the saved, but it seems I shall never see him again," mourned the mother of crew member D. E. Saunders.[4]

In the ensuing weeks and months, the story slowly unfolded. The *Titanic* struck an iceberg off the coast of Newfoundland at 11:40 p.m. on April 14, 1912. At 2:20 a.m., it sank to the ocean floor approximately 12,450 feet (3,795 m) below the surface, in the ocean's bathypelagic zone.

The New York Times.

VOL. LXI...NO. 13,826.   NEW YORK, TUESDAY, APRIL 16, 1912—TWENTY-FOUR PAGES.   ONE CENT   TWO CENTS

TITANIC SINKS FOUR HOURS AFTER HITTING ICEBERG; 866 RESCUED BY CARPATHIA, PROBABLY 1250 PERISH; ISMAY SAFE, MRS. ASTOR MAYBE, NOTED NAMES MISSING

Col. Astor and Bride, Isidor Straus and Wife, and Maj. Butt Aboard.

"RULE OF SEA" FOLLOWED

Women and Children Put Over in Lifeboats and Are Supposed to be Safe on Carpathia.

PICKED UP AFTER 8 HOURS

Vincent Astor Calls at White Star Office for News of His Father and Leaves Weeping.

FRANKLIN HOPEFUL ALL DAY

Manager of the Line Insisted Titanic Was Unsinkable Even After She Had Gone Down.

HEAD OF THE LINE ABOARD

J. Bruce Ismay Making First Trip on Gigantic Ship That Was to Surpass All Others.

Biggest Liner Plunges to the Bottom at 2:20 A. M.

RESCUERS THERE TOO LATE

Except to Pick Up the Few Hundreds Who Took to the Lifeboats.

WOMEN AND CHILDREN FIRST

Cunarder Carpathia Rushing to New York with the Survivors.

SEA SEARCH FOR OTHERS

The California Stands By on Chance of Picking Up Other Boats or Rafts.

OLYMPIC SENDS THE NEWS

Only Ship to Flash Wireless Messages to Shore After the Disaster.

The Lost Titanic Being Towed Out of Belfast Harbor.

PARTIAL LIST OF THE SAVED.

Includes Bruce Ismay, Mrs. Widener, Mrs. H. B. Harris, and an Incomplete name, suggesting Mrs. Astor's.

DIGGING DEEPER

Ocean Zones

The ocean can be divided into five separate zones. The epipelagic zone extends from the surface to 660 feet (200 m) below. Light reaches through the upper part, allowing plants to grow. The next layer is called the mesopelagic zone. Here light levels fall from dim to dark as you descend to 3,000 feet (900 m). The temperature drops to 50 degrees Fahrenheit (10°C). The bathypelagic zone reaches down to 13,000 feet (4,000 m). No sunlight reaches this zone. The *Titanic* lies here. The abyssopelagic zone drops to 19,685 feet (6,000 m.) The temperature is a constant 39 degrees Fahrenheit (4°C). The hadalpelagic zone extends to the bottom of the deepest trenches at 36,089 feet (11,000 m).[5]

← *Titanic* (to scale)

Epipelagic Zone—660 feet (200 m)

Mesopelagic Zone—3,000 feet (900 m)

X Approximate depth of *Titanic* wreck ————————— Bathypelagic Zone—13,000 feet (4,000 m)

Abyssopelagic Zone—19,685 feet (6,000 m)

Hadalpelagic Zone—36,089 feet (11,000 m) ——————

The ship left behind 712 survivors and 1,517 dead.[6] The sinking on its maiden voyage of a ship described as "practically unsinkable" shook the public's faith in technology.[7] More than a century later, people are still trying to understand what happened that fateful night and what it means for us today.

A "PRACTICALLY UNSINKABLE" SHIP

The RMS *Titanic* was named after the Titans, giants of Greek mythology. RMS stands for royal mail ship, since the *Titanic* and similar ships carried British mail as well as passengers. The ship was truly titanic in size. At 882 feet, 9 inches (269 m) long and 175 feet (53.3 m) from the bottom of its keel to the tip of its funnel, it was nearly as long as three football fields and as tall as a 17-story building.[8] Its wealthiest passengers enjoyed elegant restaurants, lounges, and even a swimming pool. Two ornate grand staircases wound through the first-class decks.

First-class passengers dined on oysters, filet mignon, roast duckling with applesauce, and other delicacies. They compared the dining experience to what one would expect from a high-class hotel. "Fancy strawberries in April and in mid-ocean. The whole thing is positively uncanny. Why, you would think you were at the Ritz," observed Lady Lucy Duff Gordon, a first-class passenger who survived along with her husband.[9]

The *Titanic*'s size and luxury were even more amazing when one considers it was built starting in 1909, without the help of most modern technology. In an age before the widespread use of automobiles, it took a team of 20 horses to pull the ship's gigantic anchor through the streets. Eight workers died during the construction of the ship, and 246 were injured.

Shipbuilder Thomas Andrews designed the *Titanic* with the very latest in safety features. The ship's hull was divided into 15 compartments. Watertight dividing walls, or bulkheads, would allow up to four of the compartments in the hull to flood without sinking the ship.

Andrews originally planned for 64 lifeboats but only ended up with 20

Many families were separated during the loading of the lifeboats.

because the ship's owners did not want the deck to look cluttered. This was more than legally required but still only enough to hold 1,178 people—approximately half the number aboard when the ship sank.[10] The ship's designers believed the ship would act as its own lifeboat, remaining afloat long enough for help to arrive. As the *Titanic* set out on April 10 on its maiden voyage from Southampton, England, to New York City, few passengers knew or cared about the lack of lifeboats.

ANATOMY OF A DISASTER

Four days into the journey, everything went wrong. Even though he received at least six warnings about icebergs in the area, Captain Edward Smith kept steaming ahead at 22.5 knots, which is approximately 26 miles per hour (42 kmh), perhaps trying to arrive in New York ahead of schedule.[11] One of the ship's lookouts, Frederick Fleet, could not find his binoculars. The sky was dark and the sea calm. Fleet did not see the looming ice until it was too late. Despite his desperate call to the bridge and a sharp turn, the huge ship could not maneuver quickly enough to avoid the ice completely. The *Titanic* grazed the iceberg, which cut a gash into the ship's hull. At least six of its compartments began to flood—too many for it to stay afloat.

Once it became clear the ship would sink, Captain Smith ordered the lifeboats loaded. However, many passengers refused to get in at first. Some felt safer on the ship, and others did not want to leave their families. Filmed versions of the *Titanic* story have shown the third-class passengers as being locked down below, but this is inaccurate. In reality, many third-class passengers simply had trouble finding their way to the upper deck from their rooms several levels below. The first lifeboats lowered were less than half full. Tradition dictated women and children should be saved first, but some men were allowed into boats to help row or fill seats if there were no women or children nearby. All in all, only approximately 700 of the 1,178 lifeboat seats were filled.[13]

THE BAND PLAYED ON

Members of the ship's band played cheerful music to help calm people as the ship slowly sank. "It did much to keep up the spirits of everyone and probably served as much as the efforts of the officers trying to prevent panic," said Hilda Slater, who escaped in the last lifeboat to leave the ship.[12]

According to *Titanic* legend, the last song the band played was the hymn "Nearer, My God, to Thee," although some historians disagree. This song was carved on bandmaster Wallace Hartley's tombstone. All eight musicians perished and were hailed as heroes.

In 2013, bandmaster Wallace Hartley's violin was discovered in an attic in England. It was reported it had been strapped to him in its case and was likely pulled from the sea along with his body. Experts believe it to be genuine.

A TALE OF TWO CAPTAINS

One of the great heroes of the *Titanic* story was Captain Arthur Rostron of the *Carpathia*. Rostron raced toward the *Titanic* as soon as he received word of the disaster, dodging icebergs along the way. Thanks to his quick actions, more than 700 lives were saved.[14]

The *Californian* was considerably closer to the sinking *Titanic*. But Captain Stanley Lord missed the *Titanic*'s frantic calls for help because his wireless telegraph operator had gone to bed. He received reports of distress rockets but did not attempt to approach the *Titanic* until hours later. He was vilified by the press and spent the rest of his life trying to explain his actions.

As the lifeboats were loaded, the ship's crew signaled frantically with their wireless telegraph and shot off distress rockets. Two ships were within range of the wireless signal, and some historians believe there was a third ship nearby as well. The closest ship, the *Californian*, did not respond. The *Carpathia* raced almost 58 miles (93 km) to the *Titanic* but arrived too late to save any people not already in lifeboats. The ship sank quickly, leaving many people floating in the icy water. Nearly everyone who did not reach lifeboats died of hypothermia.

The United States and the United Kingdom held inquiries to try to learn what happened the night the *Titanic* sank. Stories of heroes and villains emerged, and eyewitnesses gave conflicting accounts. Despite the worldwide interest and determined search for answers, the *Titanic* would keep many of its secrets hidden for the next 73 years.

THE LOCATION OF THE *TITANIC*

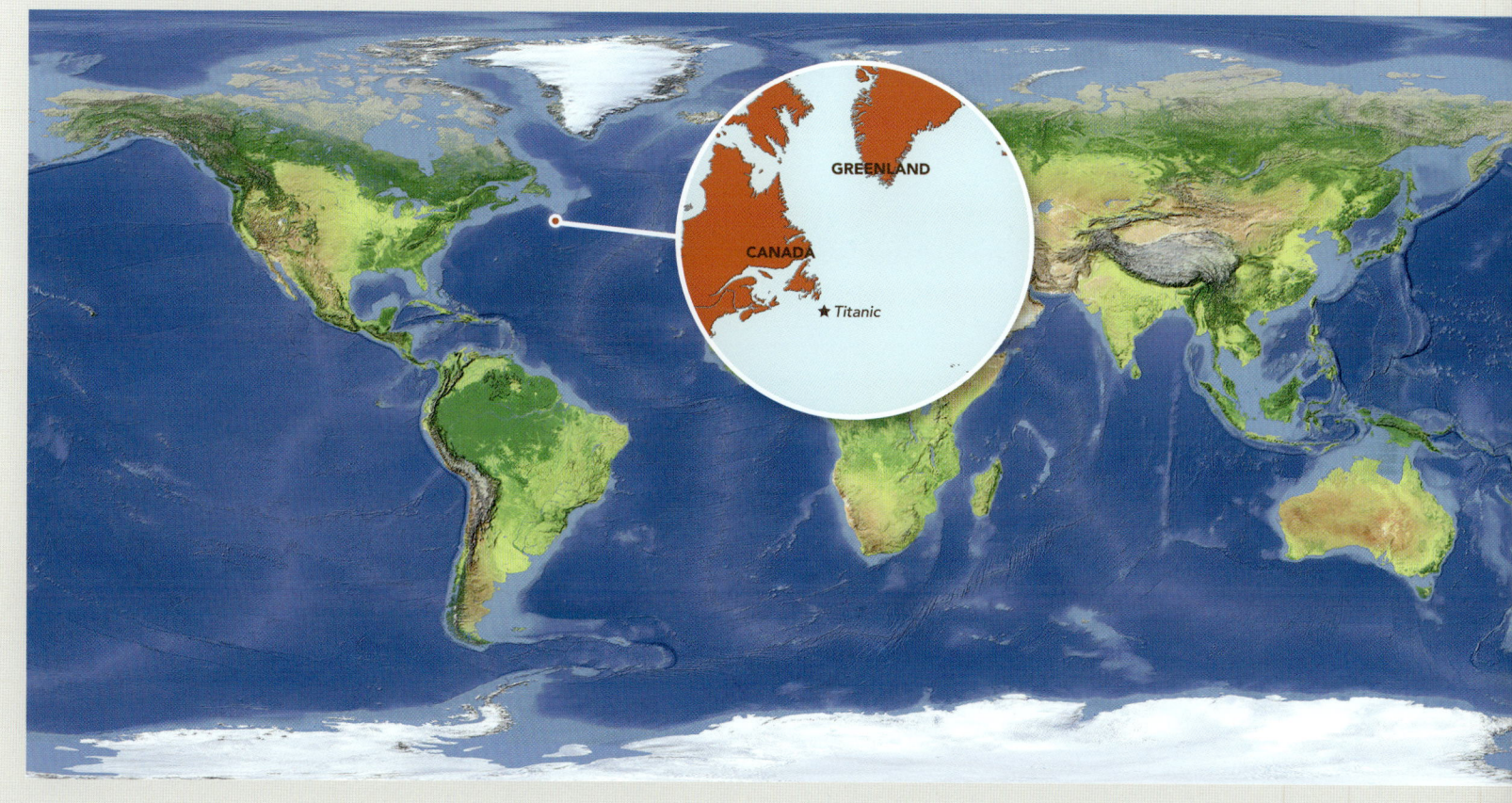

GREENLAND

CANADA

★ Titanic

The Search Begins

News of the tragedy had scarcely reached land before people started making plans to raise the *Titanic*. They ignored the fact that the technology to find the ship did not yet exist. Many believed the *Titanic* had sunk in one piece. They thought a lack of oxygen and the near-freezing temperatures on the ocean floor would have preserved it perfectly. Raising the wreck sounded difficult, but possible.

People who planned to raise the *Titanic* intact did not realize the ship had broken into pieces, making the endeavor impossible.

DIGGING
DEEPER

Early Ocean Exploration

Early divers hunting for shells, sponges, or pearls held their breath while diving to depths of approximately 100 feet (30 m). Some breathed through reeds or air-filled bags. The invention of diving bells in the 1500s let divers stay under a little longer. They swam back to the bell every few minutes to breathe the air trapped inside it.

By the 1930s, special suits, helmets, and air hoses let divers descend to 200 to 300 feet (60 to 90 m). But no one could figure out how to go deeper. Then two men had a new idea. William Beebe and Otis Barton created a diving ball called a bathysphere. They climbed inside and sank 1,426 feet (435 m) into the ocean.[1] Crew members aboard their boat used strong

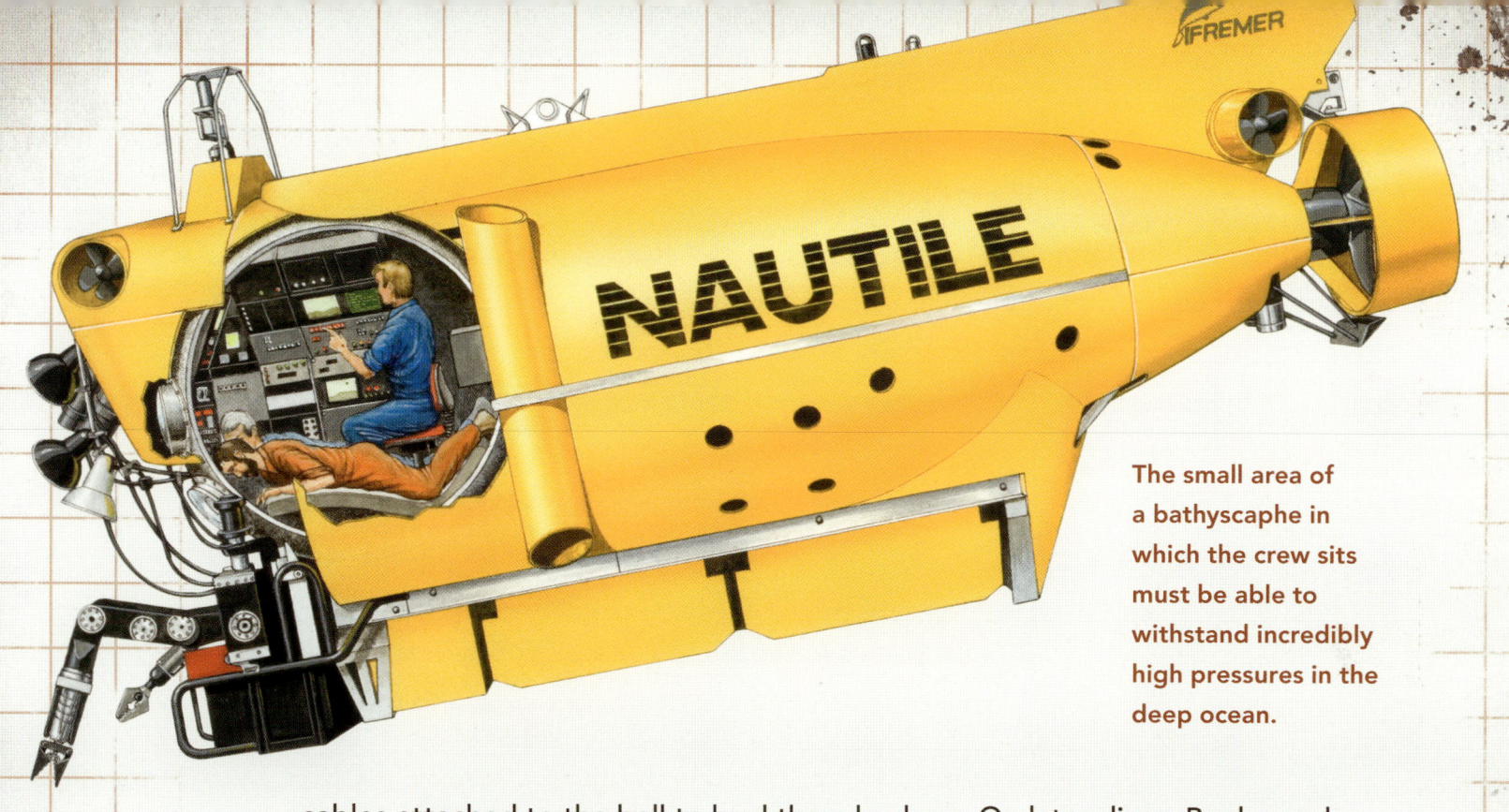

The small area of a bathyscaphe in which the crew sits must be able to withstand incredibly high pressures in the deep ocean.

cables attached to the ball to haul them back up. On later dives, Beebe and Barton reached a record 3,028 feet (923 m).[2]

The trouble was that it took a lot of power to lift the heavy bathysphere, and a broken cable meant certain death. In 1948, Swiss physicist Auguste Piccard came up with an even better idea: pull the ball down instead of up. His bathyscaphe was buoyant. Weights dragged it down and then were released when it was time to ascend. His son Jacques Piccard continued his work, eventually taking the bathyscaphe *Trieste* down to 35,800 feet (10,911 m).[3] These and many other scientists paved the way for the vehicles that finally discovered and explored the *Titanic*.

"A plan to blow up the wreckage of the *Titanic* with a powerful explosive in order to recover the body of John Jacob Astor . . . is being seriously considered to-day by Vincent Astor, son of the late Colonel," announced the *New York Evening Journal* on April 20, 1912.[4] Wrecking company owner I. J. Merritt said the plan to recover the millionaire's body was feasible. The only difficulty would be locating the ship. He proposed to sink up to 400 pounds (180 kg) of an explosive known as gun cotton and set it off.[5] This, he felt certain, would bring the bodies to the surface. Astor's body was found in the ocean shortly afterward, however, and the plan was scrapped.

Later that year, the Astors and two other wealthy families who had lost loved ones on the *Titanic* hired a wrecking company to find and raise the ship. But reality soon set in as they realized the technology of the time was not up to the task.

After that, there was little talk of finding the ship until 1953. That year, a marine salvage firm spent time near where it believed the wreck was located.

STRANGE SCHEMES

Over the years, people thought up many different ways of raising the *Titanic*. These ranged from reasonable to downright bizarre. Some people wanted to lift the ship with magnets, floats filled with helium or gasoline, or a giant claw or scoop. Others suggested filling the hull with Ping-Pong balls, Vaseline, ice, or wax to float the vessel to the surface.

The company tried to map the seafloor and locate the *Titanic* using the echoes of explosions. Nothing came of the effort.

A British court awarded British *Titanic* enthusiast Douglas Faulkner-Woolley ownership of the wreck in the 1960s, and Faulkner-Woolley still maintains this claim. In 1970, he formed a *Titanic* salvage company. It was his first of several unsuccessful attempts to recover the ship.

THE SEARCH TURNS SERIOUS

People continued devising wild schemes to raise the *Titanic* during the 1970s, even though the ship had not even been located yet. However, as deep-sea technology improved, some serious scientists began believing it might be possible to find the ship. One of these was Dr. Robert Ballard, a marine geologist who worked at the Woods Hole Oceanographic Institution in Massachusetts.

"The first time I thought it might be possible to find the *Titanic* was in 1973, when I was a member of the *Alvin* team," Ballard later wrote.[6] Although *Alvin*, a three-person submersible vehicle, could only dive to 6,000 feet (1,800 m), the US Navy was working on a new titanium hull. This extremely strong metal would make it possible for the sub to dive to 13,000 feet (4,000 m). The upgrade was called Project Titanus.

"Titanium, Titanus, *Titanic*—that started me thinking," Ballard remembered. "The *Titanic* was thought to lie at a depth of just over 12,000 feet [3,658 m]. I suddenly realized that I could dive to the *Titanic* in *Alvin*! Now thoughts of the *Titanic* just wouldn't leave me alone. I knew I had to find that ship."[7]

> "[The seafloor is] the most hostile environment known to man. Descending to those depths, with those immense pressures, presents a technical challenge that surpasses the challenge of traveling into space, with its absence of pressure. That's why mankind walked on the moon almost two decades before we were able to perform work at the bottom of the ocean."[8]
>
> —PAUL-HENRI NARGEOLET OF THE FRENCH RESEARCH INSTITUTE FOR EXPLOITATION OF THE SEA

Ballard got his first shot at the *Titanic* in 1977 when he led an expedition on behalf of Woods Hole aboard the *Alcoa Seaprobe*. The *Seaprobe* was a research drill ship, but instead of a drill, it carried a search pod. The pod held sonar equipment along with video and still cameras. Crew members attached pipes to it one at a time to increase its depth until the pod reached the ocean floor. This was a long, slow process.

Unfortunately, just as the search began, the pipe broke. Three thousand feet (900 m) of pipe and $600,000 worth of borrowed search equipment plunged to the bottom of the ocean. Ballard's

Grimm, *center*, may have nearly found the wreck, but weather, inexperience, and other factors prevented him from succeeding.

reputation took a hit, and Woods Hole withdrew its support for the search.

But Ballard did not let that stop him. He and several others formed a company called Seaonics International. Their goal was to raise money "to build deep-towed visual-imaging vehicles and find the *Titanic*." However, no one seemed willing to invest the $1.5 million they needed.[9]

THE RACE IS ON

Several others searched unsuccessfully for the *Titanic* during this period, but Jack Grimm, a Texas oil tycoon with a passion for exploration, probably came closest to finding it. Although he used the best equipment available and hired top scientists, his three expeditions in the early 1980s were cursed with bad weather. Grimm also did not search as thoroughly as he should have. Instead, he wasted valuable time following his hunches.

Grimm likely never got closer than 1.5 miles (2.4 km) from the wreck, according to Ballard. Nevertheless, Grimm maintained that a grainy photo from his 1981 trip showed one of the *Titanic*'s propellers. Grimm and company later sued for the rights to salvage the ship.

EXPLORER EXTRAORDINAIRE

Jack Grimm was perhaps the most colorful of all the *Titanic* hunters. The Texas oil tycoon spent a good portion of his life following his passion for exploration. As a boy, he once bought some dynamite and blew up a creek bed in search of Spanish gold. He found only a few arrowheads, some bullets, and a frying pan, but that was enough to "hook my imagination," he later recalled.[11] Grimm searched not only for the *Titanic*, but also for Sasquatch, the Abominable Snowman, the Loch Ness monster, and Noah's ark. He died of cancer in 1998, confident he had found both the ark and the *Titanic*.

THE DREAM THAT WOULDN'T DIE

Ballard continued dreaming about finding the *Titanic*. His dream was fueled by discussions with his friend Bill Tantum. Tantum's encyclopedic knowledge about the ship earned him the nickname "Mr. Titanic."[10] Meanwhile, Ballard stayed busy exploring other deep ocean zones for Woods Hole.

In 1979, Ballard came up with a plan for a robotic deep-sea sled with video cameras attached. Sleds are steel-framed unmanned vehicles towed along the seafloor. Cables connect the sled to the surface ship so video can be viewed in real time. This vehicle would be ideal for finding shipwrecks. It eliminated the difficulty and danger of sending humans down. Now Ballard had the dream, the skills, and the plan. All he needed was a few million dollars and backing from a major institution to search for the ship.

FABULOUS FINDS

Ballard was already an experienced deep-sea explorer by the time he started searching for the *Titanic*.

In 1973, Ballard became the first American to dive into the mid-Atlantic ridge in the French bathyscaphe *Archimède*.

Four years later, he co-led an expedition to explore the seafloor near the Galapagos Islands in *Alvin*. The scientists found giant white clams, enormous tubeworms, and other previously unknown life-forms living near hydrothermal vents. At these locations on the ocean floor, underwater volcanoes heat seawater.

Ballard was also part of the team that discovered black smokers in the East Pacific Ocean in 1979. These undersea geysers spewed 662 degree Fahrenheit (350°C) black sulfide steam from deep inside the earth and nearly melted *Alvin*![12]

3

Opportunity Knocks

In 1980, the US Navy gave Ballard the funding to develop his deep-sea video sled idea. He gathered a team of scientists at the Woods Hole Deep Submergence Laboratory to design a 15-foot (4.6 m) sled called *Argo.* It would carry sonar equipment and video cameras. A thin cable would connect it to the mother ship. A smaller tethered robot named *Jason* would carry lights and more cameras. *Jason* could explore riskier places, gather specimens, and take close-up pictures. The names of *Argo* and

Argo was capable of diving 20,000 feet (6,000 m) below the surface.

Jason came from Greek mythology. In Greek myths, the ship *Argo* and its crew of Argonauts sailed off in search of the prized Golden Fleece with the brave, handsome Jason at its helm.

This equipment would play a very important role in the discovery of the *Titanic*. Another key was Navstar, a network of global positioning system satellites that makes it possible for a ship to pinpoint its location at any given moment. New technology now made finding the ship a real possibility at last.

A SECRET MISSION

Finally, in 1985, Ballard got his long-awaited second chance. The US Navy asked him to test the new *Argo-Jason* system on the *Scorpion*, a nuclear submarine that sank in 1968. His secret mission was to find out what caused the sub to sink and gauge the condition of its nuclear reactor. When he finished the mission, Ballard could use any remaining time to search for the *Titanic*. The search was undertaken at the height of the Cold War, an ideological conflict between the United States and the Soviet Union. The search for the *Titanic* would be used as a cover story to prevent the Soviet Union from learning about the nuclear reactor search. This part of the story remained a secret for more than 20 years.

Ballard had already taken *Argo* out to sea in 1984 in a secret mission to explore another sunken submarine, the *Thresher*. It worked perfectly.

ROBERT BALLARD

It is little surprise that a man whose childhood hero was Captain Nemo, the hero of Jules Verne's legendary underwater adventure novel *20,000 Leagues under the Sea*, grew up to become one of the best-known undersea explorers of his time. "Fortunately, when I told my parents, they didn't laugh at me," Ballard recalled in an interview. "They actually encouraged me to live my dream."[1]

Growing up in California, Ballard loved to watch the sea creatures in tide pools, and he learned to scuba dive in his teens. He studied chemistry and marine geology in college in the 1960s and later did graduate work in marine geology while working as a porpoise trainer. He joined the US Navy in 1965 and was assigned to Woods Hole.

SPLIT IN HALF

Jack Thayer, who survived the *Titanic's* sinking by clinging to an overturned lifeboat, wrote later that he saw the ship break in half as it sank. Such a split would likely spread debris over a large area, which is indeed what happened. The debris field for the *Titanic* covers 15 square miles (39 sq km).[2] Thayer's words encouraged Ballard and his partners to look for a debris field instead of the ship itself, which ultimately led to their success.

The surface ship *Knorr* towed the sled over the wreckage in a careful pattern. *Argo's* cameras took photos of the downed sub and its debris field. They showed the *Thresher's* nuclear reactor safely buried in the muddy seafloor. Debris lay scattered in a pattern that looked like a comet's tail. The heavier items had sunk quickly, while lighter ones drifted in the currents. Studying this pattern gave Ballard a vital clue to finding sunken ships. Instead of searching for the ship itself, he could make wide sweeps across the ocean floor to find the debris field. Then he could simply follow the debris back to its source.

To locate the *Titanic*, Woods Hole teamed with the French Research Institute for Exploitation of the Sea (IFREMER). They planned a two-phase search effort. The search began aboard the French research ship *Le Suroit*, led by Jean-Louis Michel. Ballard and Michel had carefully studied survivors' accounts, ship logs,

Designed to carry out a wide assortment of deep-sea experiments and explorations, *Le Suroit* was built in 1975.

and newspaper clippings about the *Titanic*. They plotted out a primary search area of approximately 130 square miles (340 sq km) and a secondary area of 200 square miles (520 sq km).[3]

The researchers scanned the search area with their advanced sonar system. The system used sound waves to create images of the seafloor that looked almost like photographs. Ballard described the process as "a bit like towing a kite on a two-and-a-half mile [4 km] string."[4] The search was unsuccessful, however. Because of rough seas, *Le Suroit* was only able to cover approximately 70 percent of the search area before it had to return to port.[5]

Ballard, *center*, and his crew pored over charts and video monitors during the hunt for the *Titanic*.

Several days later, Ballard's crew set out aboard the US research vessel *Knorr* to find and explore the *Scorpion*. They were given three weeks to complete the mission. The *Scorpion* was quickly located and mapped. Now 11 days remained to hunt for the *Titanic*. They could only hope it would be enough time.

Michel and two other French team members joined the crew of the *Knorr* to continue the search for the *Titanic*. With so few days left, Ballard and Michel applied the lessons learned from the *Thresher* and *Scorpion* about debris field patterns. They would stop looking for the ship itself and instead search for the debris field with *Argo*'s video cameras. They narrowed the search field to 50 square miles (130 sq km) and began sweeping in lines one mile (1.6 km) apart.[6]

THE DISCOVERY

Crew members took four-hour shifts in the control room, watching the muddy ocean floor slide across their video screens hour after tedious hour. Their hopes dimmed as time passed. In just four days, the *Knorr* would have to return home.

On September 1, Michel and the graveyard shift had settled in for another long night of watching mud when suddenly, just before 1:00 a.m., Stu Harris pointed to the screen. A crewmember ran to wake Ballard as man-made

items appeared. The crew broke into cheers and laughter. Then a huge boiler filled the screen. Michel quickly found a picture of the *Titanic*'s boilers. It was a perfect match. "The boiler for me was the signature image that told us we'd found the *Titanic*," Ballard said later.[7]

Soon the ship itself appeared. The celebration continued until someone pointed to the clock. It was a sobering reminder that at nearly the same hour more than 70 years earlier, the *Titanic* had sunk and taken more than 1,500 lives with it. The site was truly a graveyard. Crewmembers filed out to the deck for an impromptu memorial service. They raised the flag of Harland & Wolff, the shipyard in Belfast, Ireland, that had built the *Titanic*.

Argo observed the wreck several times that day, confirming the ship had indeed broken into two pieces as it sank. But then bad weather set in, making it impossible to use *Argo* anymore. Frustrated, Ballard and Michel lowered an older, tougher sled, the *Acoustically Navigated Geological Underwater Survey (ANGUS)* in an effort to get some good photos. *ANGUS* took only still photos rather than video. The photos came out blurry, however, and only a few hours remained. So exhausted after four days without sleep that he had to lie down in the control room to keep from falling over, Ballard ordered one more set of passes with *ANGUS*. The crew positioned the sled 13 feet (4 m) above the wreck and got some clear photos just in time.[8]

The *Titanic* lies 12,450 feet (3,795 m) below the surface of the ocean, near an area known as Titanic Canyon. *Le Suroit* had come within 3,300 feet (1,000 m) of finding the wreck. It lay in a narrow section of the primary search area. Strong currents there had prevented the French from searching in the location.

SALVAGING THE *TITANIC*

An interviewer once asked Ballard what he thought about the salvaging of the *Titanic*. He replied, "I have no problem with people visiting *Titanic*. But you don't go to Gettysburg with a shovel. And you don't take belt buckles off the *Arizona*. I have no artifacts—none—nor do I want any. It's all about respect."[9]

Though disappointing to the French members of the team, their work in eliminating more than 70 percent of the search area made it possible for the *Knorr* to find the *Titanic* in the short time allowed. Ballard and Michel shared the credit for the discovery as coleaders of the expedition.

According to maritime law, the team could have claimed the right to salvage the ship by removing even a single artifact. Instead, they chose to take only photos. Even a piece of the *Titanic*'s cables accidentally snagged by *ANGUS* was tossed back, despite the fact that it would have been quite valuable to collectors. "Fortune hunting was not why we visited," Ballard wrote. "Unwilling to take any part of the ship, we threw the cable overboard."[10]

As word of the discovery got out, the world clamored for its first glimpse of the *Titanic* in 73 years. Woods Hole was not prepared for the media frenzy that followed and made some missteps. Although a joint release of photos to the French and American media was planned, Woods Hole caved to media pressure. The American media released the photos before the French could do so. This caused a serious rift between IFREMER and Woods Hole that affected their relationship for years to come.

ANGUS's rugged steel frame protects it from jagged rocks on the seafloor.

4

Return to the *Titanic*

Soon after finding the *Titanic*, the US Navy asked Ballard to return with the manned submersible *Alvin* and a small remotely operated vehicle (ROV) called *Jason Jr.* The navy planned another secret mission to further explore the *Scorpion*. The *Titanic* would serve as *Jason Jr.*'s practice run.

Alvin has made more than 4,000 deep-sea dives.

The US Navy had given Woods Hole's Deep Submergence Laboratory $2.8 million to develop *Argo* and *Jason*. After *Argo*'s success in finding the *Titanic*, DSL's next development was *Jason Jr.* Approximately the size of a lawn mower, *Jason Jr.* could fit through the *Scorpion*'s hatches to survey the inside of the sunken submarine. It carried lights and cameras but no arms to pick up or retrieve objects. *Jason Jr.*'s 250-foot (76 m) tether let it explore areas too difficult or dangerous for *Alvin* to reach.[1]

No one had ever used an ROV or fiber-optic cables at such depths before. If successful, *Jason Jr.* would open up new worlds to science. The trip to the *Titanic* would be a perfect test before the crew headed out to explore the *Scorpion*.

BALLARD RETURNS

By July 1986, Ballard was ready to return to the *Titanic* with *Alvin*, *Jason Jr.*, and the research ship *Atlantis II*. The French did not join the expedition this time, despite efforts to repair relations between the two countries' ocean research organizations. That left *Alvin* without a backup sub in case anything should go wrong. The worst-case scenario would be getting tangled in the wreckage, leaving the crew stranded on the ocean floor. Fortunately, *Jason Jr.* could explore the most dangerous areas while *Alvin*'s crew watched from a safe distance. A cable cutter was available to cut the ROV free if necessary.

The red-and-white *Alvin* submersible holds a pilot and two scientists. On July 13, 1986, Robert Ballard, Ralph Hollis, and Dudley Foster climbed inside and prepared for their long ride to the ocean floor. It would take two and a half hours to descend approximately 2.5 miles (4 km).[2] "We were like three sardines in a spherical can," wrote Ballard later. "During the long hours in the tiny cabin, my legs often fell asleep, and sometimes I'd get a bad cramp in my hip. At times like that, *Alvin*'s cabin was more like a torture chamber than a space capsule."[3]

Everything seemed to go wrong during the first dive. *Alvin*'s sonar stopped working on the way down, leaving the crew to rely on instructions from the *Atlantis II*. An alarm began blaring, indicating salt water was leaking into the

FAST FACTS ABOUT *ALVIN*

It costs approximately $40,000 per day to operate *Alvin*. This hefty price tag includes the use of its mother ship *Atlantis II* and its crew.[4]

Built by the US Navy in 1964, *Alvin* is one of the oldest research submersibles in the world. Its first triumph was locating a missing hydrogen bomb in 1966.

Alvin can descend to nearly 15,000 feet (4,500 m). The trip takes two hours each way, and the average dive lasts from six to ten hours.[5]

In 1967, a swordfish attacked *Alvin*. The unfortunate fish got tangled in *Alvin's* hull and could not escape. The crew later ate it for dinner.

battery. Then to top it all off, the sonar on the *Atlantis II* mother ship quit working. This meant the crew was driving blind——they had no way to tell which direction the *Titanic* lay. They would need to surface soon to take care of the leak. It was beginning to look like a wasted dive.

Finally, the sonar on the *Atlantis II* came back online and showed the wreck lying approximately 50 yards (46 m) west of *Alvin*. As *Alvin* moved in that direction, a hulking wall of rusted steel rose out of the gloom. The crew had time for only a quick look before surfacing for repairs. "All we had to show for six hours' work was a brief glimpse of the *Titanic*," wrote Ballard. "But my dream had finally come true."[6]

A SECOND LOOK

The following day's dive went much more smoothly, and the *Alvin* crew was able to get a good look at the *Titanic* for the first time, along with many photos. The ship appeared to be coated in rust. "Just imagine going over the top of the *Titanic* with a giant helicopter and pouring out molasses that looks like rust, and have it just pour down and over the decks and down the side of the ship," Ballard said. "It's amazing! What we thought was growth—[we] couldn't understand what kind of growth it would be, is rivers, literally rivers of rust."[7] The rust trickled down the sides of the ship and flowed out into a stream of rust on the ocean floor. Ballard coined the term *rusticles*, a combination of *rust* and *icicles*, to describe the thick, ropy growths.

The *Titanic*'s bow had sunk more than 60 feet (18 m) into the mud. It would never be possible to pull the ship out. Both anchors hung from the sides of the bow, and the bronze base that once held the ship's wheel still stood on the bridge. The wooden deck had been almost completely eaten away by wood-boring organisms. However, many portholes were intact, as were many of the thousands of objects littering the debris field—dishes, bathtubs, suitcases, wine bottles, pots and pans, and more. A light fixture still dangled near the grand staircase.

Formations of rust, described by Ballard as rusticles, covered the ship's surfaces.

TAKE IT OR LEAVE IT?

Ballard's team again chose not to salvage any artifacts from the wreck. Although Ballard had told the US Congress in 1985 that artifacts in the debris field should be recovered, he changed his mind after discussions with historians and others. The details of life in 1912 were already well-known. Besides, many survivors felt salvage would be a form of grave robbery. In the end, Ballard and the crew decided not to take anything from the wreck site.

Their resolve was tested, though, when *Alvin* came upon a locked safe in the debris field on the ocean floor. Slowly, *Alvin*'s claw reached out to turn the handle—but it would not open. Later video footage showed the bottom had rusted out. Any treasure that had once filled the safe was probably gone.

While *Alvin* took nothing from the wreck, it did leave behind one thing. The sub's mechanical arm gently released a plaque over the stern of the *Titanic*, where terrified passengers had gathered in the ship's final moments. The plaque read, "In memory of those souls who perished with the *"Titanic"* April 14/15, 1912. Dedicated to William H. Tantum, IV whose dream to find the *"Titanic"* has been realized by Dr. Robert D. Ballard, the officers and members of the *Titanic* Historical Society Inc. 1986."[8] As Ballard left the *Titanic* behind, he hoped respect for the gravesite would allow the ship to rest in peace.

WHAT HAPPENED TO THE BODIES?

The only sign of human remains found through 2013 is pairs of shoes lying together on the ocean floor. It appears their owners were still wearing them when they landed. Fish and other sea creatures likely consumed the flesh and bones. Ocean salts would have gradually dissolved the clothing and any remaining bones. Only the shoes survived, because the leather had been treated with a preservative.

Salvage Begins

As it turned out, the *Titanic* did not rest in peace for long. A group of American and European investors formed a company called Titanic Ventures to begin salvaging the ship in 1987. The previous expedition had not taken artifacts, so the company saw an opening to make money by removing items from the seafloor. Former car salesman George Tulloch headed the company. IFREMER provided the research vessel *Nadir*, the submersible *Nautile*, the ROV *Robin*, and technical support. Their

Even those in favor of salvaging items from the *Titanic* criticized a dramatic televised unveiling of artifacts from the ship.

THE *TITANIC'S* YOUNGEST SURVIVOR

The youngest *Titanic* survivor was two-month-old Millvina Dean, who was lowered to the lifeboat in a canvas mailbag. Her mother and two-year-old brother also survived, but her father went down with the ship. The Deans had hoped to open a tobacco shop and build a new life in the United States. After the disaster, the family returned to England aboard the *Adriatic*. Millvina Dean passed away in 2009 at age 97. She was the last living *Titanic* survivor.

participation was crucial. Although Ballard's team had kept the ship's location secret from the world after the first two expeditions, its French codiscoverers knew where it lay.

On their first visit to the wreck, Titanic Ventures brought up approximately 1,800 artifacts in 32 dives.[1] A television program called "Return to the *Titanic* . . . Live" followed the expedition. Accompanied by uniformed guards, host Telly Savalas opened a safe and leather bag brought up from the wreck containing banknotes and jewelry. The highly theatrical production was criticized as insensitive toward the tragedy of the *Titanic*'s sinking.

Items brought up in 1987 were displayed in France, Sweden, and Norway between 1990 and 1992. In 1992, the French government offered survivors and their heirs the opportunity to buy back artifacts with proof of ownership. According to French law, this was a necessary step before Titanic Ventures could take possession of them.

CRITICS AND COURT BATTLES

From the beginning, the salvage efforts were controversial. Survivor Eva Hart, who was just seven years old when the *Titanic* sank, was one of the most vocal critics. "To bring up those things from a mass sea grave just to make a few thousand pounds shows a dreadful insensitivity and greed," she told reporters. "The grave should be left alone. They're simply going to do it as fortune hunters, vultures, pirates!"[2] Ballard

Ballard spoke out against plans to exploit the wreck of the *Titanic* for profit.

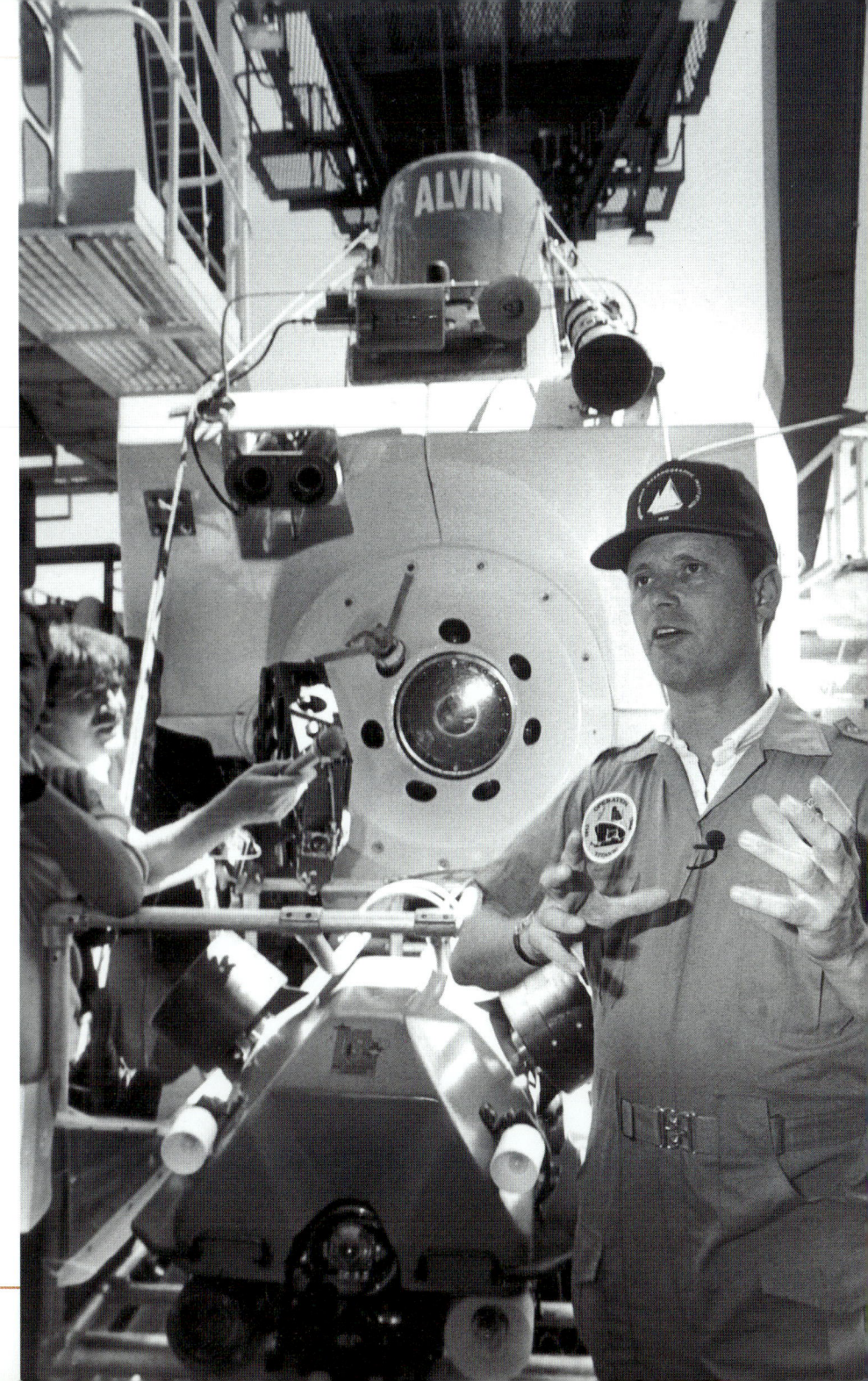

strongly denounced the salvage of the wreck as well. He felt it should be treated as a memorial to those who died there.

While they did conserve the artifacts well, the company appears not to have followed the usual archaeological practice of documenting the location of each artifact, or at least it has not made that information public. National Oceanic and Atmospheric Administration (NOAA) director of maritime heritage Dr. James Delgado was the first independent archaeologist to dive to the wreck. He wrote after his dive in 2000:

> *Despite claims by salvagers that their work is archaeologically based, it becomes obvious that they have been highly selective in what they retrieve. . . . We see scoop marks that show where selected pieces have been plucked from clusters of artifacts—no grids, no scientific sampling—simply for their display or monetary value. What is happening here, two and one-half miles [4 km] down and out of sight of much of the world, is not archaeology.[3]*

On the other hand, the salvagers argue the wreck is quickly deteriorating and will soon be nothing more than a rusty stain on the ocean floor. They view the careful preservation of artifacts as opening a window on history so future generations can better understand the *Titanic* and its times. "We need a guardian for this wreck," Tulloch said in 1996. "We need somebody to protect this maritime heritage, and we need someone to care about the archaeology. It's a piece of our history, and it's just special in every direction."[4]

Court battles began almost immediately as well. Because Titanic Ventures was the first to bring up artifacts, they were awarded the salvage rights to the ship. However, others, including one of the original British companies that insured the *Titanic*, contested their claim. These lawsuits were later dismissed.

RMS TITANIC, INC.

In 1993, Titanic Ventures reorganized and became RMS Titanic, Inc. (RMST). They returned to the wreck that year, recovering approximately 800 additional objects.[5] Also in 1993, artifacts salvaged from the *Titanic* were first put on display in the United States. RMST made additional salvage trips in 1994, 1996, 1998, 2000, and 2004, bringing up more than 5,500 artifacts in all.[6]

Since the courts have not permitted RMST to sell artifacts, the company has had to find other ways to make money. In recent years, its focus has begun shifting from salvage to science. RMST's 1996

MARINE SALVAGE

Laws about marine salvage, the process of recovering someone else's ship or cargo that is in peril or lost at sea, basically boil down to finders, keepers, Ballard says. These laws are based on the idea the people recovering the ship are putting themselves in danger and should be appropriately rewarded. The ship's owners initially own all salvage rights; however, if they make no salvage efforts, or if a long time passes with no salvage attempts, someone else can become the salvor-in-possession by recovering objects from the wreck.

expedition was the first to include serious scientific exploration. A team of naval architects, underwater imaging experts, historians, microbiologists, and archaeologists participated. Their first task was to figure out what kind of damage the iceberg had caused. To answer this question, *Nautile* carried a device called a sub-bottom profiler to the ocean floor. Its sonar let scientists peer through the mud to the *Titanic*'s hull. Instead of the long gash that many had imagined, they found only six thin slits totaling approximately 12 square feet (1.1 sq m).[7]

The next question was whether the tragedy could have been prevented. Two naval architects from the company that built the *Titanic*, Harland & Wolff, used a computer model to test different scenarios. They found that if the *Titanic* had struck the iceberg head-on instead of turning to the side, it might have survived. They also determined that if it had been moving at half its 22.5-knot (42 kmh) speed, the damage would have been far less. The *Titanic* would likely have made it to New York.

The scientists then brought up samples of steel from the ship's hull. Tests showed they contained impurities that could have made them shatter more

RMST has salvaged artifacts large and small from the *Titanic*.

easily under freezing conditions. Experts will likely never know for certain whether this affected the ship's breakup or not. Some contend that because the *Titanic*'s sister ship *Olympic* continued running on the North Atlantic until being retired in 1935, the steel may not have been a factor.

Using truck-size machines that tow lights through the water, researchers carefully studied the highly damaged stern of the *Titanic* for the first time. Engineers tried to reconstruct what happened. They determined the two halves of the ship likely broke apart at the surface. The bow sank down and landed on the ocean floor relatively intact, though the back end collapsed on impact. The stern probably ruptured from the intense pressure of the air trapped inside.

LIGHTS, CAMERA, ACTION!

Filmmakers quickly realized the world's fascination with the *Titanic* was a potential goldmine. The most prolific was James Cameron, who made four movies about the ship. He first visited in the mid-1990s while filming his blockbuster *Titanic.* "For me, filmmaking comes out of my desire to explore unknown worlds," he said. "I wanted to dive the wreck more than I wanted to make the movie. Diving the wreck was my way into the story."[8] Cameron chartered the Russian research vessel *Akademik Keldysh* and its two submersibles, *Mir I* and *Mir II*, to visit the wreck. His film *Titanic* was released

in 1997. The movie included real footage from the wreck. It cost $200 million to make but remains the second-highest-grossing motion picture of all time.[9] Only Cameron's 2009 movie *Avatar* has surpassed it. The movie greatly increased worldwide interest in the ship and its artifacts.

In 2001, Cameron returned to the *Titanic* to film the documentary *Ghosts of the Abyss*. A team of historians and scientists accompanied him. His brother, Mike Cameron, created two new ROVs to explore the ship. These boxy blue and green camera robots were nicknamed *Jake* and *Elwood*.

With their long cables, they could move around inside the wreck and peer into previously unexplored areas. The little bots almost seemed to have personalities. "The vehicle is not unlike a little creature," said Mike Cameron. "It's got a brain, it's got a computer on board; it's got eyes, in a couple cameras up front. It's got this character about it that's alive."[10]

Jake and *Elwood*'s cameras revealed cut glass windows in the ballroom that had survived their tumble to the ocean floor. Leaded glass windows in the first-class dining room were still intact as well. Molly Brown's famous brass bed, Henry Harper's bowler hat, and the elegant elevator doors were a few of the other items found.

After two movies, James Cameron still was not finished with the *Titanic*. "I feel like I've lived on *Titanic*, certainly much longer than any of the people who were actually involved in the event did," he said. "I've got it ingrained in my memory. I could walk the ship in my sleep."[11] He returned to the wreck in 2005 for yet another documentary, *Last Mysteries of the Titanic*. Then in 2012, he assembled a team of forensic experts

THE *TITANIC* AND HOLLYWOOD

The first film about the sinking of the *Titanic* opened just 29 days after the tragedy. It was the 1912 short silent movie *Saved from the Titanic*, starring survivor Dorothy Gibson. The American film star played a fictional version of herself, reportedly wearing the same clothes she had been rescued in.

to produce *Titanic: The Final Word with James Cameron*. In this movie, the experts explored some of the unanswered questions about *Titanic*, using footage from previous dives, deck plans, and survivor testimonies to create a new visualization of the sinking.

JAKE AND *ELWOOD*

Jake and *Elwood* were named after characters in the 1980 film *Blues Brothers*. Engineer Mike Cameron wanted to create ROVs that could safely explore the interior of the ship without getting tangled in debris and exit at a different point than they entered if necessary. He came up with a robot that could spin out a thin fiber-optic tether the width of fishing line, just like a spider spinning its web. It carried its own power supply and could move up to 2,000 feet (610 m) away from the sub.[12] If a bot got stuck, as did indeed happen, it could just spin out more line and keep going. The bots are controlled with a helicopter-style joystick. Since exploring the *Titanic*, *Jake* and *Elwood* have gone on to explore the German battleship *Bismarck* and mid-Atlantic hydrothermal vents. The US Navy is also exploring their potential for underwater recovery of ships and aircraft.

Mapping the Site

Although Ballard expected his 1986 visit to the *Titanic* to be his last, 18 years later he returned with a NOAA expedition. Concerned about the condition of the ship, he wanted to document its deterioration. He also hoped to promote the ship's preservation and show the world a way to appreciate the *Titanic* without removing artifacts. The National Geographic Society, an educational organization, filmed the trip for the documentary *Return to Titanic.* "I wanted to make Titanic a test case for dealing with the

Mapping and scanning technology improved dramatically in the years since Ballard's first expedition.

thousands of shipwrecks still lying unexplored in international waters," Ballard later wrote. "That was a tall order, but one I relished."[1]

Technology had come a long way since Ballard's previous visit to the *Titanic.* This time there was no need for humans to dive on the wreck. Instead, an ROV called *Hercules* and the *Argus* sled were lowered from NOAA's research vessel, the *Ronald H. Brown.* The research vessel holds spacious laboratories and advanced sonar to map the ocean floor in three dimensions. A global positioning system linked to thrusters on its stern and bow can park the ship at an exact point on the ocean surface.

Hercules carries its own set of thrusters, along with lights and cameras. It attaches to the *Argus* sled, a more advanced version of the *Argo* sled used in 1985. The name *Argus* also comes from the Greeks; the mythological Argus built Jason's ship. *Argus* carries strong lights, and a fiber-optic cable connects it to the *Ronald H. Brown.*

LOOK, BUT DON'T TOUCH

NOAA directed the team to "look, but don't touch." It was allowed to only pick up rusticle experiments left during previous visits and set up two new

Hercules helped provide the best images yet of the *Titanic.*

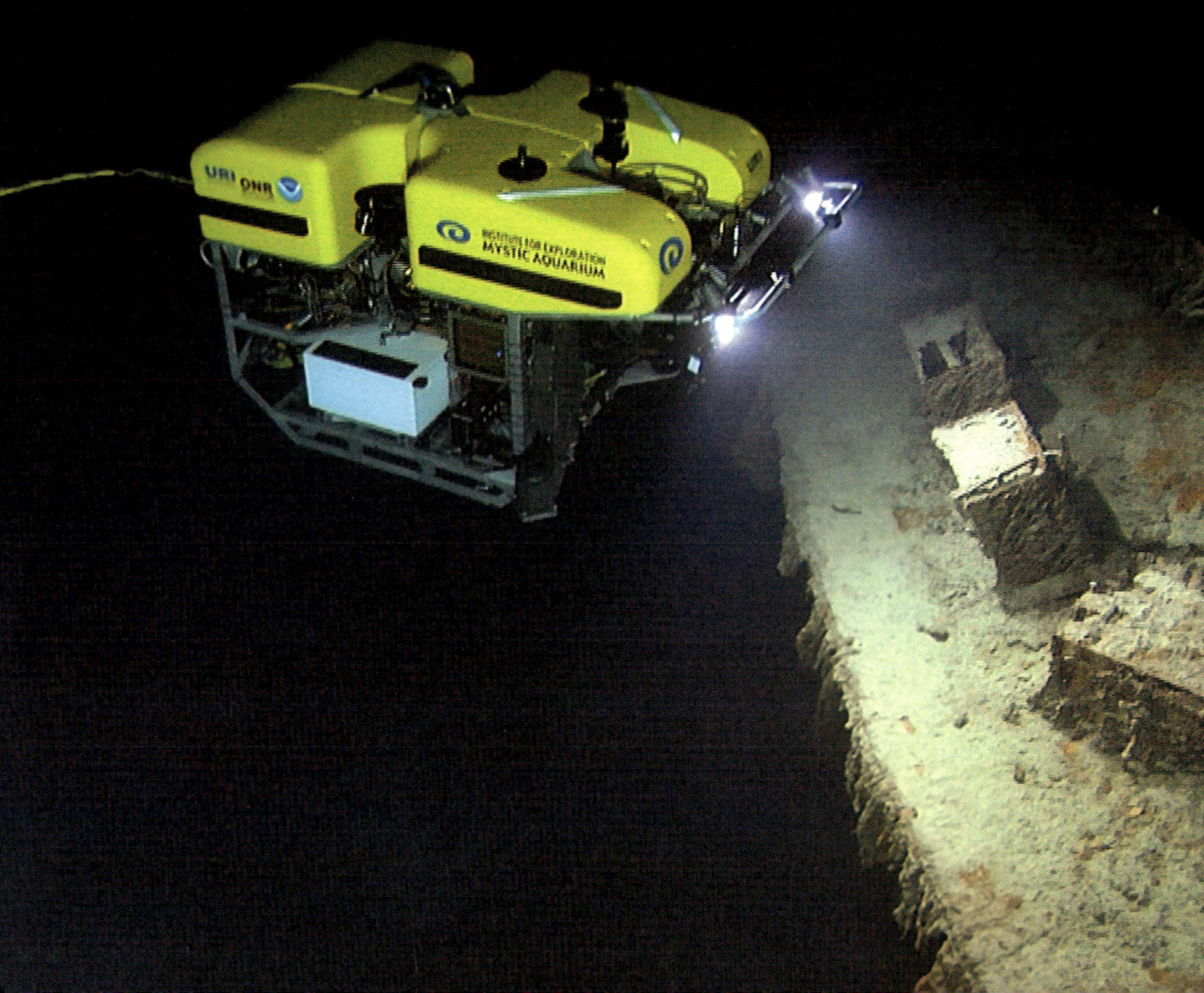

scientific platforms. Once it reached the site of the wreck, *Hercules* began moving in a pattern above it, pausing every few seconds to snap a photo. The ROV moved neatly through a preprogrammed course plotted out on a three-dimensional grid. It sent back high-definition photos and video of the wreck and surrounding area.

Manned submersibles are heavy and clumsy and can easily damage a shipwreck when they bump into or land on it. *Hercules*'s footage revealed damage to the wreck from previous submersible visits—holes, bends, sagging walls, and marks in the sand. Garbage from surface ships had found its way to the bottom, along with pieces of tangled cable and other debris from HOVs. Damage to the mast and the device that once held the wheel was also seen.

Hercules's photos were carefully stitched together to form a detailed photomosaic of the wreck site. "If seeing is believing, then witnessing such a legendary expanse of steel beneath the *Ron Brown* erased any doubts that remotely operated vehicles could do all that submersibles could do, and more," wrote Ballard. "Our *Hercules*, like the mythological Greek hero who completed 12 seemingly impossible labors, had succeeded beyond the power of imagination."[2]

RMST CHANGES COURSE

RMST invited a group of unlikely partners to join its eighth expedition in August 2010. These included Woods Hole, the Waitt Institute, NOAA, the National Park Service, and others. Some of them had harshly criticized RMST for their salvage methods in the past. No items were to be salvaged this time, though. The goal of the expedition was to create detailed maps of the complete wreck site. While thousands of photos had been taken over the years, no one had ever systematically mapped the entire site. This information would be useful not only for scientists studying the *Titanic* but also for policymakers.

RMST seems to have changed course entirely with this trip. "For years, the only thing that all the voices in the *Titanic* community could agree on was their disdain of us," said Chris Davino, RMST president since 2009. "So it was time to reassess everything. We had to do something beyond artifact recovery. We had to stop fighting with the experts and start collaborating with them."[3]

BURIED TREASURE

Many have speculated about buried treasure on the *Titanic*. Although wealthy passengers brought jewelry and cash along, the ship's cargo was valued at only $420,000. Despite a rumored shipment of diamonds worth $300 million today, salvage operations so far have turned up only a bag of passengers' jewelry, cash, and coins.[4] A court barred RMST from cutting into the wreck in 2000, so searchers will likely never know for sure.

FROZEN IN TIME

The images made at the wreck site are valuable resources for future *Titanic* scholars. "As a scientist, I appreciate the way these photographic documents freeze concrete images of *Titanic* at specific points in time," wrote Dr. Ballard in his book *Return to Titanic.* "They provide crucial data for those who wish to preserve the great ship: objective, precise observations instead of rumor and anecdote. The fact that the [images] are beautiful artwork in their own right is a bonus."[6]

The team set out in the research vessel *Jean Charcot*. Between three hurricanes, they managed to map the site with a new type of autonomous underwater vehicle (AUV). AUVs are not connected to cables. They can dive to nearly 20,000 feet (6,100 m) and run for up to 22 hours.[5] Each holds several types of sonar, cameras, and sensors. The team's yellow torpedo-shaped AUVs, dubbed *Ginger* and *Mary Ann*, surveyed the wreck site using sonar.

In addition, an ROV with lights and cameras collected high-quality images. The sonar and photo mosaics were later combined to create a detailed, accurate picture of the wreck site. Since Woods Hole has data on the site going back more than 25 years, scientists can now get a much clearer picture of changes over time.

"This is a game-changer," said Delgado about how the new technology changed the work at the shipwreck. "In the past, trying to understand *Titanic* was like trying to understand Manhattan at midnight in a rainstorm—with a flashlight. Now we have a site that

can be understood and measured, with definite things to tell us."[7] Or, as Bill Lange of the Woods Hole Advanced Imaging and Visualization Laboratory put it, "After a hundred years, the lights are finally on."[8]

7

Artifacts and Displays

Since 1987, RMST has carefully removed more than 5,500 artifacts from the *Titanic* wreck site, ranging from postcards to a 15-short-ton (13.6 metric ton) chunk of the ship's hull. The company has preserved them and exhibited them around the world. RMST's goal is to conserve the artifacts before bacteria, sediments, salts, and acids in the ocean destroy them along with the ship itself.

Artifacts from the *Titanic*, including the sheet music used by the ship's musicians, have been seen by museum visitors across the world.

The company collected the artifacts using the French submersible *Nautile*. Scooping, grasping, and suction devices on *Nautile*'s robotic arms can pick up anything from fragile china to giant lifeboat cranes. Small items are carried to the surface in *Nautile*'s basket. Larger items are placed in wire cages lined with foam. When a basket is full, it is released and floats to the surface. Divers attach a safety line to it and place a net over the top before it is lifted to the ship.

Lift bags filled with diesel fuel are used to raise extremely heavy items, such as the three–short-ton (2.7 metric ton) device once used for securing cables on the *Titanic*. The diesel fuel is less dense than water, so it always floats. Heavy chains pull the bags to the ocean floor, where *Nautile* attaches the bags to the artifact. When the chains are released, the object rises to the surface. The diesel fuel is then pumped back into *Nadir*'s fuel supply.

ALL KINDS OF ARTIFACTS

When the *Titanic* broke in half, passengers' belongings and the ship's furnishings poured out onto the ocean floor. RMST's first recovery mission in 1987 brought up approximately 1,800 objects. Among them were a gilded chandelier, compass, wheel pedestal, ship's bell, porthole, and leaded glass window. *Nautile* recovered the cherub that once danced at the base of the ship's Grand Staircase and 238 dishes lying neatly in rows. Their wooden case had rotted away.

Approximately 800 more artifacts were recovered during the 1993 expedition. These included one of the ship's whistles, a double lifeboat crane, and part of an engine. The ROV *Robin* was also sent out to explore the interior of the ship, including the Grand Staircase and the mailroom where sacks of mail still sat.

The following summer, RMST returned for 18 more dives that yielded a gold pocket watch, souvenir plates, and a passenger's binoculars, among other things.

SALVAGING THE "BIG PIECE"

In 1996, RMST attempted its most difficult recovery to date—a 15–short-ton (13.6 metric ton) piece of the ship's hull plating measuring 23.5 feet (7.2 m) long and 14 feet (4.3 m) wide.[1] The "Big Piece," as it was called, would be lifted with bags filled with diesel fuel. Film crews from the Discovery Channel came along to document the undertaking. Two cruise ships

UNUSUAL CARGO

Titanic's cargo manifest lists large quantities of books, boots, brandy, and other everyday items. But it carried some rather unusual cargo as well: 12 cases of ostrich feathers, four cases of opium, 19 cases of rare orchids, 16 cases of rabbit hair, and 76 cases of dragon's blood. Dragon's blood is the name for a palm fruit resin that was used to color varnish and women's makeup.

complete with casinos, Vegas-style shows, celebrities, *Titanic* survivors, and closed-circuit TVs followed. "You can't bring this thing up with no one looking. This is theater," said Tulloch, who was president of RMST at the time.[2]

While their intention was to raise money to fund the expedition, the company was criticized for creating such a circus-like atmosphere. Many felt it was disrespectful to those who died on the *Titanic*.

The operation was nearly successful. The lift bags brought the Big Piece to within 215 feet (66 m) of the surface. Then bad weather set in, snapping the ropes holding it in place. The Big Piece drifted back to the ocean floor, 10 miles (16 km) from its original position.[3] It was marked with an underwater beacon so it could be found later. A plaque dropped onto the Big Piece read, "I will come back. George Tulloch."[4]

Two years later, RMST tried again. This time, they brought no cruise ships or live audience, though the operation was made into a television special. Six lift bags brought the Big Piece to the surface, and a crane hoisted it onto the deck of a waiting ship. It was preserved and put on exhibit in Las Vegas, Nevada.

GEORGE TULLOCH

George Tulloch, the man behind RMST, was a born salesman. He sold encyclopedias in prep school and worked for another book sales company in college. Tulloch then built up a large auto dealership.

When Tulloch heard about plans to salvage the *Titanic*, he raised more than $2 million for the expedition and formed Titanic Ventures, which later became RMS Titanic, Inc. He was president of the company until a hostile takeover in 1999. Tulloch then moved on to a new project: searching for the lost city of Atlantis with a friend from the *Titanic* expeditions. Tulloch died of cancer in 2004.

VALUABLE ARTIFACTS

Most of the items recovered from the *Titanic* so far have been everyday items such as silverware, shoe brushes, and razors. Though they are common items, they are now valuable to collectors. One leather bag held 300 gold coins, diamond jewelry, gold watches, and $65,000 in cash. It likely came from a purser's safe—a place where the ship's wealthy passengers could safely stow their valuables when not wearing or using them.

Rumors of other treasures continue tantalizing treasure seekers. Records show that steward F. Dent Ray saw pursers loading valuables from the first-class safes into canvas bags, but most of these bags have never been found. Storekeeper Frank Prentice recalled loading gold and silver bars onto the ship, but there is no evidence of them on the cargo list. However, they could have been sent as mail and not listed as cargo.

BACK TO THE FAMILY

Nautile brought up a gold pocket watch that had belonged to Edith Brown Haisman's father, Thomas Brown. It was given to Edith at age 91. She kept it for the remainder of her life. The watch was then returned to RMST and put on exhibit.

Advanced salvage technology allowed workers to lift enormous pieces of the *Titanic* from the ocean floor.

FRAGILE ARTIFACTS

Many people are amazed to learn letters, postcards, and dollar bills were found intact after 75 years on the ocean floor. How could such fragile items survive? RMST says that surviving artifacts made of paper or textiles were found inside leather items, such as suitcases, trunks, or wallets. Chemicals used to tan the leather prevented the growth of microbes that would have otherwise broken down the artifacts.

One valuable item known to have gone down with the *Titanic* has never been found: a book called *The Rubaiyat of Omar Khayyam*. A special cable to the *Chicago Examiner* on April 21, 1912, announced: "A copy of the Rubaiyat of Omar Khayyam, illustrated by Elihu Vedder, which took two years to bind in very elaborate tooled morocco, inlaid with 1,500 gems and gold setting, and which was bought by an American at Sotheby's less than a month ago, was lost on the *Titanic*. The American paid $2,025 for it."[5] While that was a lot of money in 1912, it was less than the price of a first-class ticket on the *Titanic*, $2,500. The ticket would cost approximately $57,200 in today's dollars.[6]

PRESERVATION TECHNIQUES

Artifacts brought up from the ocean floor must be treated as soon as they are exposed to air. Otherwise, ocean salts may crackle ceramic glazes and destroy metal surfaces. Organic items such as paper, wood, and cloth will quickly mold or decay. As soon as artifacts are brought up, conservators place them in foam-lined tubs of fresh water and gently clean them with a soft brush. Each artifact is measured, photographed, and documented on board the research vessel.

Artifacts from RMST's first expedition were preserved by laboratories in France. There each artifact was conserved, but not restored. The goal was simply to stop it from deteriorating further. The laboratories believed artifacts would be more meaningful if displayed in the condition they were found.

The process used depends on what type of material is involved. Most items are placed in desalination baths to remove ocean salts. The liquid is changed frequently until no additional salts leach out.

Delicate items, such as a shirt belonging to a third-class passenger, require careful handling to preserve.

Electrolysis—running a small electric current through the item—removes salt from metal. Leather, paper, and wood products are treated with electrolysis as well as chemicals to remove rust and fungus.

Glass and ceramics are the simplest to conserve; after the salts are removed, they are slowly dried. Paper items, on the other hand, must be freeze-dried and then cleaned with special vacuums and hand tools. Leather and wooden items are injected with a type of wax after they are cleaned. The wax fills in spaces left by water and debris to keep the items from cracking.

Once the artifacts are conserved, they must be protected from sunlight and kept in an environment with carefully controlled temperature and humidity. Historians then work to identify them. Often they can discover who originally owned an item or which part of the ship an artifact came from.

WHO OWNS THE ARTIFACTS?

While it might seem logical to return artifacts to their owners' families, in some cases historians cannot identify who owned a particular item. If the owner is known, which descendant should inherit the item? What if descendants are hard to track down? The courts have awarded ownership of the artifacts to RMST with the condition that they cannot sell them off individually and must exhibit them to the public.

There is one exception to this rule: coal. Because of a quirk in the law, the coal spilled from the broken ship is not considered an artifact. It is not a man-made object, and it would have been burned anyway. So RMST began selling tiny chunks of coal to finance their recovery efforts. Many people jumped at the chance to own a piece of the *Titanic*. Others opposed this attempt to make money.

In 2013, the entire collection of more than 5,500 artifacts was offered for sale. They were valued at $189 million.[7] The courts agreed to allow the sale, as long as the artifacts were properly cared for, displayed to the public, and kept together.

THE *TITANIC'S* COAL

The *Titanic* was a steamship, powered by burning coal in its huge engines. It could carry 7,703 short tons of coal (6,988 metric tons), and burned 600 short tons (544 metric tons) a day in its 159 furnaces. It took 176 stokers, called firemen, to do the backbreaking, dirty job of shoveling all that coal.[8] The *Titanic's* maiden voyage was nearly delayed by a coal miners' strike that caused a shortage of coal that spring. The strike ended on April 9, but coal had to be collected from several other liners to fill the *Titanic's* bunkers. When the ship sank, several thousand tons of coal spilled out onto the ocean floor.

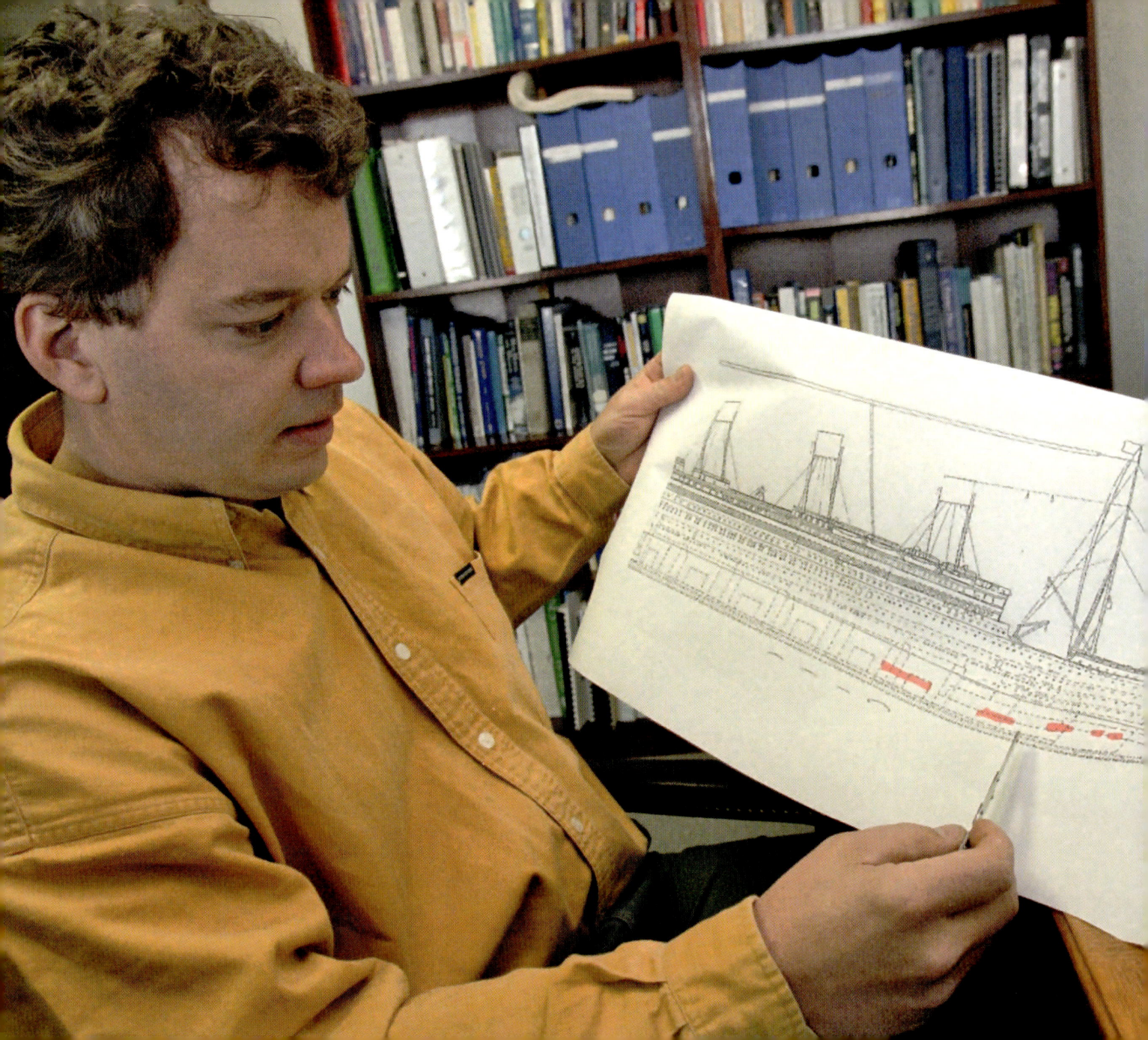

What the *Titanic* Has Taught Us

One of the first things the discovery of the *Titanic* taught us was that the ship definitely broke into two pieces as it sank. When Ballard and Michel discovered the ship in 1985, they found the bow and stern lying a third of a mile (0.5 km) apart.[1]

The discovery that several small holes, rather than one large one, sank the *Titanic* challenged a common belief about the ship more than 80 years after its sinking.

This finding confirmed Jack Thayer's and other survivors' accounts of the ship breaking in two as it sank. It also explained why the debris field is so large: items literally poured out of the two halves of the ship as it sank. The artifacts fanned out widely during the ship's 2.5 mile (4 km) tumble to the ocean floor. The resulting 15-square-mile (39 sq km) debris field helped Ballard and Michel find the wreck in 1985.

Ever since the ship was found, scientists have been debating exactly how and why it broke apart. Initial tests found that perhaps the steel used to make the 3 million rivets holding the ship together contained impurities. This could make them turn brittle in extremely cold conditions. The steel would snap instead of flexing as it should. Later researchers did not find this to be a fatal flaw, however.

A number of *Titanic* survivors testified they saw the ship break in two. Several of these said it broke at a low angle instead of tilting nearly upright, as often pictured. Naval architect Roger Long suggested the design of the expansion joints—spaces left between sections so the ship could flex slightly between waves—may explain why the ship broke at a low angle. After the *Titanic* sank, shipbuilders redesigned the joints on its sister ship, the *Britannic*.

The ship's breakup resulted in a large debris field, helping searchers find the wreck.

They may have feared the joints were to blame for the breakup. However, Long concluded the *Titanic* was fine for everyday service. The forces acting on it as it sank were simply so great something had to give.

During the making of his documentary *Titanic: The Final Word with James Cameron*, the filmmaker and a team of experts came up with a new theory of how the ship broke apart. Using computer modeling, they showed it likely split from the top down. The double hull on the bottom of the ship hung together until finally the pressure tore it apart.

THE "HOLE" TRUTH

In 1996, scientists were able to peer through the mud using a sub-bottom profiler carried by *Nautile*. It formed a sonar picture of the buried hull. The results showed the iceberg did not cut a 300-foot (91 m) gash, as was commonly believed. Instead, it cut six thin slits that, added together, were about the size of a human body. "It wasn't very impressive. But it was impressive enough to sink the ship," said Ballard in a 2012 documentary.[2]

Astonishingly, this was precisely what naval architect Edward Wilding had concluded a century ago. Based on survivors' testimonies and reports on the flooding pattern, he figured out a long gash would have sunk the ship in just minutes. He said the total area damaged could have totaled no more than approximately 12 square feet (1.1 sq m).[3] With no computers, sonar or other high-tech tools, Wilding was remarkably close to the truth.

UNLOCKING PASSENGERS' LIVES

"The goal of marine archaeology is to better understand the past; in particular, human beings in the past, through what's left behind," said Delgado. "Everything that was enclosed in that ship, now spread out on the sea bed, tells us about them."[4] The artifacts left behind give us a glimpse into the everyday lives of the passengers and crew on the *Titanic*—their food, clothing, toys, and tools. Their letters even tell us what they thought about.

Many of the third-class passengers on the *Titanic* were immigrating to the United States. They would have packed their most treasured possessions in their trunks. Most of them owned very little. The average passenger carried two pieces of luggage: a carpetbag or trunk with clothing and personal items for the voyage and another to be stowed below, in the hold. However, wealthy first-class passengers sometimes

A *TITANIC* BACTERIUM

In 2010, previously unknown deep-sea bacteria identified in samples of rusticles from the *Titanic* were named *Halomonas titanicae* in honor of the ship. *H. titanicae* is one of 27 different strains of bacteria that live together and form rusticles.[5]

brought many more. Mrs. James Warburton Martinez Cardeza of Pennsylvania, for example, traveled with her son and maid. They brought along 14 trunks, four suitcases, and three crates of baggage.

THE *TITANIC* IS DISINTEGRATING

Some were surprised to see the poor condition of the artifacts inside the *Titanic*. Many people expected the ship to be perfectly preserved due to the expected lack of oxygen and extreme cold on the seafloor. This was not an unreasonable idea. Some very well-preserved wrecks have been found over the years. Divers even discovered intact jars of food in a 2,000-year-old Roman ship in 2012.

But the conditions in the area where the *Titanic* sank are much harsher. Iron-eating bacteria are gradually dissolving the wreck. Its exposed wooden parts have already been eaten away by other organisms. Salt water and

High-quality imagery has made possible exhibits like the one shown in Northern Ireland in 2012, in which visitors could look through a glass floor onto projected views of the *Titanic*'s wreck beneath them.

MIRAGES

New revelations continue to be made about the circumstances surrounding the *Titanic* disaster. In 2012, British historian Tim Maltin suggested that atmospheric conditions might have been responsible for the sinking. By studying survivors' testimonies, ship logs, and weather records, he learned that the layers of warm and cold air caused mirages that night. This optical illusion may have hidden the iceberg until it was too late. It may also have distorted the *Titanic's* signals and distress rockets.

sediments continue wearing away at the ship and artifacts. No one knows for sure how much longer the wreck will last.

TECHNOLOGICAL ADVANCES

The *Titanic* has taught us much about life at 12,450 feet (3,795 m) under the sea, but one of its most important contributions to science is the new deep-sea technology it spurred. The public's fascination with the wreck provides ongoing funding and motivation for researchers to return again and again. It keeps pushing technology to the next level, giving us an ever-clearer picture of the scene. Recent expeditions showed that unmanned vehicles work well for exploring the ocean floor. They can operate either remotely or by themselves. Unmanned vehicles are much smaller and easier to maneuver than HOVs, and they do less damage to the wreck site. In the case of an accident, no lives are at stake.

Underwater imaging technology has also improved since 1985, partly because the world was so anxious to see photos and video of the *Titanic*. Ballard's idea of putting a live video feed on *Argo* was groundbreaking. It worked so well that engineers soon developed new and improved deep-sea cameras. The newest three-dimensional cameras let viewers feel like they are actually at the scene.

"Designing a deep-sea camera system is a lot more than just taking a camera off the shelf and putting it in a pressure-resistant tube," said Lange. "There's a lot of engineering that goes into making these cameras work efficiently at depths of more than 13,000 feet [4,000 m], withstand pressures of 10,000 pounds per square inch [700 kg per sq cm] and a range of temperatures from 100°F [38°C] on deck to near freezing on the seafloor; operate on really low power; and produce high-optical-resolution images in very low light levels."[6] Since there is not a big market for this type of camera, you cannot just buy one off the shelf.

As scientists and filmmakers continue visiting the *Titanic*, they create a record of how the wreck has changed over time. This information can be applied to other shipwrecks. The equipment designed to explore the *Titanic* will allow scientists to explore other deep-sea areas in the future as well.

The Future of the *Titanic*

Between human interference with the wreck and natural decay, the future of the *Titanic* is uncertain. "The danger lies not in man's greed but in his curiosity," wrote *Titanic* historian Walter Lord in 1986.[1] The world's curiosity about the *Titanic* has led to many scientific advances, but it has caused damage to the wreck site as well.

Some expeditions to the *Titanic* have left plaques as a memorial to the victims of the tragedy.

Ballard and others argue humans are destroying the monument the site could and should be. "The *Titanic* is really a deep-sea museum—with the doors wide open," said Ballard. "There's no lock on the door and there's no guard."[2]

Besides the items legally recovered by RMST, other artifacts have disappeared. As ROVs become more common, it is becoming easier for pirates to loot the wreck. Tourism is increasing as well—one couple even got married in a submersible on the wreck.

LAYING DOWN THE LAW

Lawmakers have tried to protect the wreck over the years. Soon after the *Titanic*'s discovery, US President Ronald Reagan signed the RMS Titanic Maritime Memorial Act of 1986. The act made the *Titanic* into an international memorial. However, the *Titanic* lies in international waters, so US law alone could not protect it. That would take an international agreement. The United Kingdom, France, and Canada did not seem interested at the time.

By 1995, the four countries began discussions. In 2000, they laid out a draft agreement. RMST sued to prevent them from doing this, but the lawsuit was dismissed. In 2012, the wreck fell under the protection of the United Nations Educational, Scientific and Cultural Organization (UNESCO). This means that from now on, United Nations members protect the ship and ensure any human remains are treated with dignity. They can seize illegally taken artifacts and prohibit anyone from selling or destroying artifacts.

Forty-one countries signed the agreement. The United States and Canada were not among them, but they did sign an "International Agreement Concerning the Shipwrecked Vessel *RMS Titanic*," known as the *Titanic* Agreement, in 2003. France and the United Kingdom also signed the agreement, which is similar to the UNESCO agreement.

RMST has now reversed its earlier position on salvaging the wreck and supports creating a protected *Titanic* memorial. It is working with other agencies on guidelines to protect the ship. Dave Conlin, chief marine archaeologist at the US National Park Service, applauds the company for its new approach.

The fragile remains of the *Titanic* are now protected by international agreements.

"RMST deserved the flak they got in years past, but they also deserve credit for taking this new leap of faith," he said.[3]

PRESERVING THE *TITANIC*

Ballard is dreaming of bigger and better things for the *Titanic* these days. One idea is to provide video cameras that would monitor the site at all times. A live, continuous broadcast could be made available on the Internet. The site could become a virtual museum. Visitors would simply log on to their computers to view the wreck in real time.

Ballard also suggests scraping and painting the hull of the ship to stop further decay. While it sounds far-fetched, it is already being done to other ships in shallower waters. Magnetic underwater robots regularly clean and paint the hulls of supertankers. They apply a special thick paint that prevents rust.

The *Titanic* Advisory Council is working on additional guidelines for protecting the site. One idea is to create a no-litter zone so ships cannot dump waste around the wreck site. Another is to designate

NO REGRETS

Ballard was once asked whether he ever regrets finding the wreck. "No," he said. "The *Titanic* is critical because people are fascinated by it, and will listen to the call to preserve it. . . . We can use *Titanic* as a platform to present our case that the deep sea is the biggest museum of the world. It has more artifacts in it than all the museums of the world combined. . . . We need to generate international laws to protect human antiquity."[4]

entry and exit points for submersibles. This would prevent them from dropping their weights in the artifact field.

CHANGING THE FUTURE

The *Titanic* has taught us much about marine archaeology. The public's interest in the wreck provides money for new equipment and scientific studies. The debate over how to manage the wreck will help researchers and lawmakers decide how to handle such sites in the future.

Approximately 14 large ships sink each year, and many times the cause is a mystery.[5] Techniques used in studying the *Titanic* will help researchers of the future solve these cases. Some of the sunken ships contain hazardous waste or tanks of oil. Studying the *Titanic* is teaching us more about how shipwrecks decay and how to prevent their dangerous cargoes from damaging the environment.

Deep-sea technology continues improving. High-tech imaging and unmanned vehicles mean humans no longer need to visit the ocean floor to get a clear picture of what is going on. The urge to visit wrecks in person is lessened when amazing imagery can be beamed to the safety of the surface. New three-dimensional cameras will allow scientists to view and measure shipwrecks and artifacts without ever seeing or touching them. And many more people will be able to study them this way.

THE *TITANIC* LIVES ON

Scientists disagree how much longer the *Titanic* will last. Some think it will collapse soon, while others think it will be there for centuries. But all agree it will eventually break down. Regardless, the *Titanic* will live on in our imaginations for many years to come. This century-old drama has not yet come to an end.

It is hard to say exactly why the *Titanic* still captivates the world more than a century after it sank. The blend of glamour, technology, and human drama may have been the key to capturing people's imaginations. Filmmaker James Cameron believes the story of the *Titanic* forces people to consider how they might react to the sinking: "Until our lives are really put at risk, the moment of truth, we don't know what we would do," James Cameron said.[6]

Whatever the reason, the world's interest in the *Titanic* has taught us much about the disaster itself. Studying the wreck has helped open up undersea worlds we could only dream of exploring 30 years ago. And the *Titanic* still has much to teach us as we continue unlocking its mysteries.

Public fascination with the *Titanic* continues more than a century after the famous ship slipped beneath the icy waters of the North Atlantic.

TIMELINE

1909

Construction of the *Titanic* begins. It becomes one of the largest and most luxurious ocean liners ever made.

1912

On April 10, the *Titanic* sets sail from Southampton, England.

1912

On April 14 at 11:40 p.m., Frederick Fleet spots an iceberg. He rings the ship's bell and alerts the bridge. It is too late. Just 37 seconds later, the *Titanic* grazes the iceberg.

1912

On April 15 at 2:18 a.m., the ship snaps in two and the bow sinks. The stern follows a few minutes later.

1985

On September 1, the wreck is discovered by a joint French-American expedition under the leadership of Robert Ballard and Jean-Louis Michel.

1986

In July, Ballard and crew return to the *Titanic*. They explore and photograph the entire wreck in a manned submersible.

1987

In August, Titanic Ventures, along with IFREMER, the French codiscoverers of the wreck, visit the ship and begin recovering artifacts.

1998

RMS Titanic, Inc. successfully retrieves the Big Piece and puts it on display.

2004

Ballard returns to the wreck to document the deterioration of the *Titanic*.

2009

The last known *Titanic* survivor, Millvina Dean, dies at age 97.

2010

RMS Titanic, Inc. partners with NOAA, the Waitt Institute, and others to perform a detailed wreck site survey.

2013

The entire *Titanic* collection is offered for sale.

DIGGING UP THE FACTS

DATE OF DISCOVERY

The wreck of the *Titanic* was first spotted on September 1, 1985.

KEY PLAYERS

- Dr. Robert Ballard, a marine geologist at Woods Hole Oceanographic Institution, was a codiscoverer of the wreck.

- Jean-Louis Michel, an oceanographer and engineer with IFREMER, was a codiscoverer of the wreck.

- George Tulloch, a former car salesman, was president of salvage company RMS Titanic, Inc.

- James Cameron, filmmaker and *Titanic* enthusiast, created films and documentaries about the ship.

- Chris Davino is the current president of RMS Titanic, Inc.

KEY TECHNOLOGIES

Sonar made it possible to see through murky seas. Submersibles, such as *Alvin*, allowed scientists to visit the *Titanic* in person. ROVs, such as *Argo*, *ANGUS*, and *Jason Jr.* made exploring the wreck safer.

IMPACT ON SCIENCE

The world's interest in the *Titanic* has advanced marine archaeology in many ways. Scientists created new deep-sea cameras to photograph the wreck and new vehicles to explore it. The debate over salvaging the wreck has helped establish policies for managing marine archaeological sites in the future.

IMPACT ON CULTURE

The *Titanic* is unquestionably the most famous shipwreck in history. It was well known in the decades after the sinking, but Robert Ballard's 1985 discovery of the ship's resting place brought it back into the public consciousness. A little more than a decade later, the incredible success of James Cameron's film *Titanic* not only proved there was a continued interest in the ship, but also ensured it will remain famous for years to come. Since the film's release, dozens of popular documentaries, television shows, books, and museum exhibits have shown people are still fascinated by the *Titanic*'s mysteries.

QUOTE

"The *Titanic* is critical because people are fascinated by it, and will listen to the call to preserve it. . . . We can use *Titanic* as a platform to present our case that the deep sea is the biggest museum of the world."—*Robert Ballard*

GLOSSARY

boiler
A tank in which water is heated to create steam to power an engine.

bow
The front end of a ship.

bridge
A raised platform from which the ship is navigated.

bulkhead
A wall that separates compartments inside a ship.

compartment
A section inside a ship that is divided off by walls and doors.

funnel
A pipe or chimney that allows smoke to escape.

hull
The frame or body of a ship.

keel
A structure running down the center of the bottom of a boat that helps keep the vessel stable.

maiden voyage
A ship's first trip.

rivet
A metal pin used to fasten two pieces of metal together.

salvage
To save a ship or its cargo from loss at sea.

sonar
A device that finds objects underwater using sound waves.

stern
The back end of a ship.

submersible
A vehicle that travels underwater.

ADDITIONAL RESOURCES

SELECTED BIBLIOGRAPHY

Ballard, Robert D. *Return to* Titanic. Washington, DC: National Geographic, 2004. Print.

Gill, Anton. Titanic: *Building the World's Most Famous Ship.* Guilford, CT: Lyons, 2010. Print.

Maxtone-Graham, John. Titanic *Tragedy: A New Look at the Lost Liner.* New York: Norton, 2011. Print.

FURTHER READINGS

Adams, Simon. *Eyewitness* Titanic. New York: DK, 2009. Print.

Denenberg, Barry. Titanic *Sinks!* New York: Viking, 2011. Print.

Vanderhook, Sue. *The* Titanic. Minneapolis, MN: ABDO, 2008. Print.

WEBSITES

To learn more about Digging Up the Past, visit **booklinks.abdopublishing.com**. These links are routinely monitored and updated to provide the most current information available.

FOR MORE INFORMATION

For more information on this subject, contact or visit the following organizations:

MYSTIC AQUARIUM

55 Coogan Boulevard

Mystic, CT 06355

860-572-5955

http://www.mysticaquarium.org

Mystic Aquarium is the home of Dr. Ballard's Institute for Exploration.

THE TITANIC HISTORICAL SOCIETY

PO Box 51053

208 Main Street

Indian Orchard, MA 01151

413-543-4770

http://www.titanichistoricalsociety.org

The Titanic Historical Society is the first and largest *Titanic* organization and maintains a museum in Indian Orchard, MA.

WOODS HOLE OCEANOGRAPHIC INSTITUTION

266 Woods Hole Road

Woods Hole, MA 02543

508-289-2252

http://www.whoi.edu

Woods Hole is a nonprofit organization that studies all aspects of the ocean.

SOURCE NOTES

Chapter 1. A Titanic Tragedy

1. Robert D. Ballard. *The Discovery of the Titanic*. New York: Warner Books, 1995. Print. 81.

2. Ibid.

3. "On This Day: 16 Apr. 1912." *New York Times*. New York Times, 2010. Web. 31 May 2013.

4. Great Lakes Science Center. "*Titanic*: The Artifact Exhibition." Cleveland, OH: Great Lakes Science Center, 2013.

5. Michael Allaby. *Dictionary of Ecology*. Oxford U P, 2010. Web. 18 June 2013.

6. "United States Senate Inquiry Report." Titanic *Inquiry Project*. Titanic Inquiry Project, 2013. Web. 31 May 2013.

7. Paul Louden-Brown. "*Titanic*: Sinking the Myths." *BBC History*. BBC, 3 Mar. 2011. Web. 31 May 2013.

8. Susan Wels. Titanic: *Legacy of the World's Greatest Ocean Liner*. New York: Time-Life, 1997. Print. 33.

9. Great Lakes Science Center. "*Titanic*: The Artifact Exhibition." Cleveland, OH: Great Lakes Science Center, 2013.

10. "History of RMS *Titanic*." *Woods Hole Oceanographic Institution*. Woods Hole Oceanographic Institution, 2013. Web. 30 Dec. 2013.

11. "*Titanic*." *Encyclopaedia Britannica*. Encyclopaedia Britannica, 2013. Web. 1 June 2013.

12. "Worcester Evening Gazette: Brave Musicians of Ship Meet Fate Trying To Drown Cries of the Perishing Passengers." *Encyclopedia Titanica*. Encyclopedia Titanica, 2013. Web. 20 May 2013.

13. "*Titanic*." *Encyclopaedia Britannica*. Encyclopaedia Britannica, 2013. Web. 1 June 2013.

14. Donald Lynch. Titanic: *An Illustrated History*. New York: Hyperion, 2013. Print. 142, 157.

Chapter 2. The Search Begins

1. Robert D. Ballard. *The Eternal Darkness*. Princeton, NJ: Princeton U P. Print. 13.

2. Ibid. 33.

3. Ibid. 55.

4. "Astor to Dynamite *Titanic*." *Encyclopedia Titanica*. Encyclopedia Titanica, 2013. Web. 29 May 2012.

5. Ibid.

6. Robert D. Ballard. *Exploring the* Titanic. New York: Scholastic, 1988. Print. 8.

7. Ibid. 9.

8. Susan Wels. Titanic: *Legacy of the World's Greatest Ocean Liner*. New York: Time-Life, 1997. Print. 161.

9. Robert D. Ballard. *The Discovery of the* Titanic. New York: Warner, 1995. Print. 41.

10. Robert D. Ballard. *Exploring the* Titanic. New York: Scholastic, 1988. Print. 9.

11. "*Titanic* at 100: Abilene's Jack Grimm Ship-finding Adventures Still Reverberate." *Abilene Reporter-News Online*. Abilene Reporter-News Online, 7 Apr. 2012. Web. 30 May 2013.

12. Robert D. Ballard. *The Eternal Darkness*. Princeton, NJ: Princeton U P, 2002. Print. 201–202.

Chapter 3. Opportunity Knocks

1. "An Interview with Dr. Robert Ballard," *Homeschool.com*. Homeschool.com, 2013. Web. 12 June 2013.

2. "*Titanic* by the Numbers." *History Channel*. History Channel, 2013. Web. 10 June 2013.

3. Robert D. Ballard. *The Discovery of the* Titanic. New York: Warner, 1995. Print. 57.

4. Ibid. 61.

5. Robert D. Ballard. *Return to* Titanic. Washington, DC: National Geographic, 2004. Print. 41.

6. Robert D. Ballard. *The Discovery of the* Titanic. New York: Warner, 1995. Print. 67.

7. *Secrets of the* Titanic: *Mysteries of the Deep*. Dir. Bob Ballard. National Geographic, 1986. DVD.

8. Robert D. Ballard. *The Discovery of the* Titanic. New York: Warner, 1995. Print. 94.

9. Jim Clash. "Robert Ballard Interview." *Askmen.com*. Askmen.com, 2013. Web. 24 May 2013.

10. Robert D. Ballard. *Return to* Titanic. Washington, DC: National Geographic, 2004. Print. 69.

Chapter 4. Return to the *Titanic*

1. Robert D. Ballard. *Return to* Titanic. Washington, DC: National Geographic, 2004. Print. 57.

2. Ibid. 58.

3. Robert D. Ballard. *Exploring the* Titanic. New York: Scholastic, 1988. Print. 38–39.

4. "Alvin FAQs." *Woods Hole Oceanographic Institution*. Woods Hole Oceanographic Institution, n.d. Web. 18 June 2013.

5. "Human Occupied Vehicle Alvin." *Woods Hole Oceanographic Institution*. Woods Hole Oceanographic Institution, n.d. Web. 30 Dec. 2013.

6. Robert D. Ballard. *Exploring the* Titanic. New York: Scholastic, 1988. Print. 40–41.

7. "1986 Return to RMS *Titanic*." *Woods Hole Oceanographic Institution*. Woods Hole Oceanographic Institution, n.d. Web. 30 Dec. 2013.

8. Robert D. Ballard. *Exploring the* Titanic. New York: Scholastic, 1988. Print. 57.

Chapter 5. Salvage Begins

1. John P. Eaton and Charles Haas. Titanic: *A Journey Through Time*. New York: W. W. Norton, 1999. Print. 194.

2. Donald Lynch. Titanic: *An Illustrated History*. New York: Hyperion, 2013. Print. 208.

3. James P. Delgado. "Diving on the *Titanic*." *Archaeology Magazine Archive*. Archaeology Magazine, Jan./Feb. 2001. Web. 5 June 2013.

4. Titanic: *The Investigation Begins*. Discovery Channel, 1996. Web.

5. John P. Eaton and Charles Haas. Titanic: *A Journey Through Time*. New York: W. W. Norton, 1999. Print. 200.

6. "RMS *Titanic*, Inc." *Premier Exhibitions*. Premier Exhibitions, 2012. Web. 10 June 2013.

7. Susan Wels. Titanic: *Legacy of the World's Greatest Ocean Liner*. New York: Time-Life, 1997. Print. 142.

8. Titanic: *The Final Word with James Cameron*. Dir. Tony Gerber. Market Road Films, 2012. Web.

9. Robert W. Welkos. "The $200-Million Lesson of 'Titanic.'" *Los Angeles Times*. Los Angeles Times, 11 Feb. 1998. Web. 4 June 2013.

10. *Ghosts of the Abyss*. Dir. James Cameron. Walt Disney, 2003. Web.

11. *Last Mysteries of the* Titanic. Dir. Neil Flagg. Discovery Channel, 2005. DVD.

12. Titanic: *The Final Word with James Cameron*. Dir. Tony Gerber. Market Road Films, 2012. Web.

Chapter 6. Mapping the Site

1. Robert D. Ballard. *Return to* Titanic. Washington, DC: National Geographic, 2004. Print. 7.

2. Ibid. 144.

3. Hampton Sides. "Unseen *Titanic*." *National Geographic Magazine*. National Geographic, April 2012. Web. 10 June 2013.

4. Ricardo J. Elia. "Diving for Diamonds." *Archaeology Magazine*. Archaeology Magazine, 20 Sept. 2000. Web. 5 June 2013.

5. James P. Delgado. "Archaeology of *Titanic*." *Archaeology Magazine Archive*. Archaeology Magazine, May/June 2012. Web. 5 June 2013.

6. Robert D. Ballard. *Return to* Titanic. Washington, DC: National Geographic, 2004. Print. 162–163.

7. Hampton Sides. "Unseen *Titanic*." *National Geographic Magazine*. National Geographic, April 2012. Web. 10 June 2013.

8. Ibid.

Chapter 7. Artifacts and Displays

1. "*Titanic*: The Artifact Exhibition Permanently Docks at Luxor Hotel and Casino." *Luxor Hotel*. Luxor Hotel, 2008. Web. 19 June 2013.

2. Stephen J. Spignesi. *The Complete* Titanic. New York: Citadel, 1999. Print. 318–319.

3. Susan Wels. Titanic: *Legacy of the World's Greatest Ocean Liner*. New York: Time-Life, 1997. Print. 166–169.

4. Stephen J. Spignesi. Titanic *for Dummies*. Hoboken, NJ: Wiley, 2012. Print. 258.

5. "$2,025 Book on *Titanic*, Special Cable to the Examiner." *Encyclopedia Titanica*. Encyclopedia Titanica, 2013. Web. 11 June 2013.

6. "*Titanic*: The Artifact Exhibition." *South Carolina State Museum*. South Carolina State Museum, 2012. Web. 30 Dec. 2013.

7. "*Titanic*: The Auction." *Guernsey's*. Guernsey's, 8 Mar. 2012. Web. 4 June 2013.

8. Anton Gill. Titanic: *Building the World's Most Famous Ship*. Guilford, CT: Lyons, 2010. Print. 152.

Chapter 8. What the *Titanic* Has Taught Us

1. "*Titanic* Is Falling Apart." *National Geographic Daily News*. National Geographic, 18 Aug. 2010. Web. 7 June 2013.

2. *Save the* Titanic *with Bob Ballard*. National Geographic, 2012. DVD.

3. Lonny Lippsett. "The Quest to Map *Titanic*." *Woods Hole Oceanographic Institution*. Woods Hole Oceanographic Institution, 12 Apr. 2012. Web. 30 Dec. 2013.

4. Titanic *at 100: Mystery Solved*. Dir. Tony Bacon. Edgeworx Studios, 2012. DVD.

5. "New Species of Bacteria Found in *Titanic* 'Rusticles'." *BBC News*. BBC News, 6 Dec. 2010. Web. 27 May 2013.

6. Lonny Lippsett. "The Quest to Map *Titanic*." *Woods Hole Oceanographic Institution*. Woods Hole Oceanographic Institution, 12 Apr. 2012. Web. 30 Dec. 2013.

Chapter 9. The Future of the *Titanic*

1. Walter Lord. *The Night Lives On*. New York: Open Road Media, 1998. *Google Book Search*. Web. 30 Dec. 2013.

2. *Save the* Titanic *with Bob Ballard*. National Geographic, 2012. DVD.

3. Hampton Sides. "Unseen *Titanic*." *National Geographic Magazine*. National Geographic, April 2012. Web. 10 June 2013.

4. Robert D. Ballard. *Return to* Titanic. Washington, DC: National Geographic, 2004. Print. 160.

5. Lonny Lippsett. "The Quest to Map *Titanic*." *Woods Hole Oceanographic Institution*. Woods Hole Oceanographic Institution, 12 Apr. 2012. Web. 30 Dec. 2013.

6. Titanic: *The Final Word with James Cameron*. Dir. Tony Gerber. Market Road Films, 2012. Web.

INDEX

ABOUT THE AUTHOR

Lisa J. Amstutz is a freelance writer specializing in nonfiction for children and adults. *The Titanic* is her sixteenth book, and her work has appeared in a variety of magazines as well. Lisa particularly enjoys discovering amazing stories and fun facts about science and history to share with kids. Her background includes a BA in biology and an MS in environmental science.